CW01456676

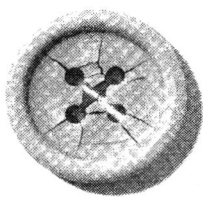

B●LD FAITH
BOLD LEADERSHIP

*A 21-Day Devotional Guide
for Christian Leaders in
an Uncertain World*

CONTENTS

Introduction

I've got this button in my desk drawer. Four holes, perfectly spaced, but utterly useless. The little cross-shaped piece in the middle snapped off years ago. I can't bring myself to throw it away, though some people would say I'm mad for keeping broken things. But that button . . . well, you'll understand why by Day 19.

Right now, you're probably wondering what a broken button has to do with bold faith or leadership. That's rather the point of this entire book, actually. God keeps showing up in the most unexpected places – in FedEx logos and French vineyards, in tree physics and the peculiar fact that "a fat chance" and "a slim chance" mean exactly the same thing. He's constantly revealing Kingdom truths through ordinary things, if we've got eyes to see them.

This uncertain world we're navigating – with its shifting values, technological disruption, cultural upheaval, and genuine global challenges – it feels like we're trying to lead (or simply live faithfully) while the ground keeps moving beneath our feet. Every week brings fresh complexity.

Yesterday's solutions become today's problems. What worked for previous generations seems almost quaint now.

But here's what I've been discovering: uncertainty isn't the enemy of faith – it's faith's natural habitat. After all, if we were certain about everything, what would we need faith for? And character isn't forged in comfort but in exactly these kinds of challenging times when the old maps don't work anymore and we have to navigate by the stars.

Whether you're leading a church, running a business, teaching a classroom, or simply trying to raise children who love Jesus in a world that increasingly doesn't – you're a leader. You're influencing someone. You're shaping the spiritual atmosphere around you. And in uncertain times, the world desperately needs leaders (that's you!) who aren't just managing institutions but demonstrating what it looks like to follow a God who turns kingdoms upside down while keeping His people right-side up.

Over the next twenty-one days, we're going on a rather unusual journey together. We'll discover why athletes understand spiritual growth better than many theologians, why being "careful" might be the opposite of what you think, and how giving away what you have creates the very vacuum that draws in more. Each day builds on the last, though you can also dip in wherever you need to.

This isn't about perfecting your leadership technique or adding more burden to your already overwhelming load. It's about seeing differently. Once you start recognising Kingdom patterns breaking through everywhere – in morning routines and evening meals, in corporate mistakes and cosmic movements – you can't unsee them. The ordinary becomes extraordinary. Everything starts preaching.

So bring your uncertainty. Bring your questions. Bring that sense that you're not quite enough for what God's called you to. Perfect! That means you're ready. Because bold faith isn't the absence of doubt – it's choosing to trust when trust seems foolish. And bold leadership isn't about having all the answers – it's about following the One who does, especially when you can't see the path ahead.

Ready? Let's discover what God's been hiding in plain sight.

DAY 1

What Wasn't in the Garden?

"He will wipe every tear from their eyes. There will be no more death or mourning or crying or pain, for the old order of things has passed away." (Revelation 21:4)

"Adam and his wife were both naked, and they felt no shame." (Genesis 2:25)

REFLECTION

I was thinking about this the other day, and it struck me quite forcefully – we spend so much time studying what was in the Garden of Eden, but have you ever considered what wasn't there? It's pretty amazing when you think about it, because sometimes the absence of something tells us more about God's original design than what was present.

Here's something that makes me chuckle: Adam and Eve didn't have belly buttons. No, really! Think about it for a moment. They weren't born, so no umbilical cords, hence no belly buttons. How many Renaissance paintings have you seen that get that detail completely wrong? Michelangelo's Sistine Chapel – brilliant as it is – shows Adam with a belly button. But that's just the beginning of what was missing.

No clothes. No fashion industry. Can you imagine? The entire global fashion industry – worth about 1.7 trillion pounds annually – simply wouldn't have existed. No agonising over what to wear. No keeping up with trends. No status symbols draped over our shoulders. They were naked and felt no shame. That's not just about physical nakedness, is it? It's about complete transparency, absolute vulnerability without fear.

But here's where it gets really interesting. There was no worry in that garden. None whatsoever. The amygdala – that almond-shaped part of our brain that processes fear and anxiety – would have functioned completely differently. Scientists tell us that chronic worry actually changes our brain structure, creating neural pathways that make us more prone to anxiety. In Eden, those pathways simply didn't exist in that way.

No death. Just sit with that for a moment. No funeral industry. No grief counselling. No life insurance. No medical intervention to stave off the inevitable. The very concept of "deadline" wouldn't have made sense. Time had a completely different quality when it stretched endlessly before you.

DAY 1

No tears of sorrow – though I wonder if there might have been tears of joy? No lies – imagine a world where every word spoken was trustworthy, where promises never needed contracts, where "yes" always meant yes. The legal profession, built largely on the reality of human deception and broken promises, unnecessary.

And this is what captures my imagination most powerfully: this garden, this perfect home, it's actually a mirror. It reflects both backwards to what we've lost and forwards to what we're heading towards. Revelation doesn't describe heaven as something entirely foreign to human experience – it describes it as Eden restored and glorified. No more tears. No more death. No more mourning or crying or pain.

You see, when God placed Adam and Eve in that garden, He was showing us His heart for humanity. The absence of all these things – worry, fear, death, deception, shame – that's not just ancient history. That's our future! That's where this whole story is heading. Every time you feel the weight of anxiety, every moment you wrestle with fear, every tear you shed in grief – these are reminders that you weren't made for this fallen world. You were made for a garden without shadows.

As leaders, we spend so much energy managing what shouldn't exist – conflict resolution, trust rebuilding, anxiety management, crisis intervention. These are necessary skills in our fallen world, absolutely. But isn't it remarkable that none of these would have been needed in God's original design? And won't be needed in His restored creation?

The garden whispers to us about who we really are and where we're really going. We're not just evolved creatures trying to survive. We're beings designed for paradise, temporarily sojourning through a broken world, but headed home to a place where belly buttons on Adam will be the least of the inaccuracies we'll laugh about.

LIVING IT OUT

Today, take a moment to identify one thing in your life that wouldn't have existed in Eden – perhaps worry about a decision, fear about the future, or shame about the past. Instead of seeing this as just another burden to bear, let it remind you that you were made for something better. This discomfort with brokenness?

That's actually your soul's memory of paradise and its longing for home. In your leadership today, speak hope into someone else's "wasn't meant to be this way" moment. Remind them – and yourself – that every absence in Eden is a promise about heaven. We're not just managing dysfunction; we're preparing people for paradise.

PRAYER

Father, thank You that the garden wasn't just history – it's prophecy. When I feel the weight of things that weren't in Eden, remind me that I wasn't made for them. They won't last forever.

Give me eyes to see past the temporary dysfunction to the eternal restoration You're preparing. Help me lead others with the hope of Eden restored, not just the management of Eden lost.

May my discomfort with this world's brokenness keep me longing for home. Amen.

TOMORROW'S PREVIEW

Tomorrow we'll explore something fascinating about creation: God didn't just create the sun and moon; He created them to rule. What does celestial governance teach us about leadership in our own spheres?

DAY 2

Sun to Rule the day

"And God said, 'Let there be lights in the vault of the sky to separate the day from the night, and let them serve as signs to mark sacred times, and days and years, and let them be lights in the vault of the sky to give light on the earth.' And it was so. God made two great lights – the greater light to govern the day and the lesser light to govern the night." (Genesis 1:14-16)

REFLECTION

Have you ever noticed that specific word in Genesis? Not just that God created the sun and moon, but that He created them to govern. To rule. The Hebrew word there is "memshalah" – it means dominion, governance, authority. Not illuminate. Not decorate. Rule.

That fascinates me.

The sun doesn't ask permission to rise. Every single morning, since its creation, it has exercised its dominion over day. It pulls our planet in a precise elliptical orbit. Without consultation or committee meetings, it drives our weather systems, powers photosynthesis, regulates our circadian rhythms. Scientists estimate the sun converts 600 million tons of hydrogen into helium every single second, releasing energy that takes 8 minutes and 20 seconds to reach us. That's governance on a scale we can barely comprehend.

And the moon! Often overlooked as the "lesser light", yet it governs our tides with such precision that we can predict them centuries in advance. It stabilises Earth's axial tilt, keeping our seasons relatively constant. Without the moon's governing influence, our planet would wobble chaotically, making life as we know it impossible. Even our word "month" comes from "moon" – it's been governing our calendars since humans first looked up.

But here's what really gets me: this was Day Four. Before God created a single human being, before He breathed His image into Adam, He established the principle of governance. Authority. Leadership. Rule.

Think about that for a moment. Leadership isn't some human invention we came up with to organise ourselves after things got complicated. It's woven into the very fabric of creation. Before there were kingdoms or companies, before there were churches or communities, there was rule. Divine order. Purposeful authority.

The sun never has an identity crisis about its role. It doesn't wake up Tuesday morning thinking, "Perhaps today I'll be the moon." It knows its assignment: rule the day. Provide light. Sustain life. Create seasons. It exercises authority without arrogance, power without pride. Just consistent, faithful, life-giving governance.

I wonder if that's why Jesus called Himself the Light of the World? Not just illumination – though He certainly brings that – but governance. Rule. Authority that brings order to chaos, life to death, hope to despair.

You know what else strikes me? The sun rules by giving, not taking. Every moment of its governance involves pouring out energy, light, warmth. It loses 4 million tons of mass every second, converted into the energy that sustains all life on earth. That's the kind of leadership written into creation itself – authority that depletes itself for the flourishing of others.

And notice – the sun and moon rule different spheres. The sun doesn't compete with the moon or belittle its "lesser" light. Each has its ordained sphere of governance. The moon gloriously reflects light it doesn't generate, and that borrowed light has guided countless travellers through history. There's no shame in reflected glory when you're fulfilling your ordained purpose.

Even their apparent exceptions teach us about leadership. Solar eclipses – those moments when the moon seems to overrule the sun – they're temporary, predictable, and ultimately serve to remind us of the normal order. Sometimes in leadership, the unusual moment, the exception, the eclipse, actually reinforces the rule.

When you step into leadership today – whether that's in your home, your church, your workplace – remember that you're not imposing some artificial human construct. You're participating in something God built into creation before He formed humanity. Governance and authority aren't necessary evils in a fallen world; they're part of the "very good" creation God designed.

The question isn't whether leadership and authority should exist – God settled that on Day Four. The question is whether we'll exercise our appointed rule like the sun: consistently, faithfully, life-givingly, each in our ordained sphere, pouring ourselves out for the flourishing of those under our governance.

LIVING IT OUT

Look at your sphere of influence today – where has God positioned you to "rule"? Perhaps it's a team at work, a ministry at church, or simply your own household. Like the sun, exercise that authority by giving rather than taking. Pour out energy that helps others flourish. Don't apologise for having authority – God built it into creation's rhythm. But remember the sun's example: it rules by serving, governs by giving, leads by illuminating the path for others. Today, identify one specific way you can exercise sun-like leadership – consistent, life-giving governance that enables others to thrive in their own ordained spheres.

PRAYER

Creator God, You established governance before You created humanity – what a profound truth! Thank You that leadership isn't a burden we invented but a pattern You wove into creation.

Help me rule my appointed sphere like the sun – faithfully, consistently, sacrificially. Show me how to exercise authority that gives life rather than takes it, that serves rather than demands, that illuminates rather than overshadows.

May my leadership today reflect Your original design: bringing order, enabling flourishing, sustaining life. Amen.

DAY 2

TOMORROW'S PREVIEW

If the sun and moon teach us about created authority, tomorrow we'll discover something extraordinary – Jesus has been given authority over everything human. Not some things. Everything. What does that mean for how we lead under His ultimate rule?

DAY 3

Authority Over All

"For you granted him authority over all people that he might give eternal life to all those you have given him." (John 17:2)

"Far above all rule and authority, power and dominion, and every name that is invoked, not only in the present age but also in the one to come. And God placed all things under his feet." (Ephesians 1:21-22)

REFLECTION

Right there in John 17, in what some call the "Holy of Holies" of Scripture – Jesus' intimate prayer with His Father – He makes this staggering claim: authority over all people. Not some people. Not religious people. Not willing people. All people.

Every. Single. Human.

Now, I find the timing of this prayer absolutely riveting. Jesus prays this hours before His arrest. Hours before religious leaders condemn Him. Hours before Pilate interrogates Him about His Kingdom. Hours before soldiers mock Him with a crown of thorns. Hours before He appears to lose everything.

And what does He pray? "Father . . . glorify your Son . . . For you granted him authority over all people" (John 17:1-2).

The irony is breath-taking, isn't it? The One claiming authority over all humanity is about to be nailed to a Roman cross by human hands. The One given dominion over every person is about to be spat upon, stripped, and seemingly defeated by people.

But that word in Greek – "exousia" – it doesn't mean the authority of force or coercion. It means the right to act, the freedom of action, the power of choice. Jesus has been given the right to give eternal life to all the Father has given Him. His authority serves one supreme purpose: giving life.

Paul, writing to the Ephesians years later, takes this even further. Actually, he goes completely cosmic with it. No name is exempt. No power stands outside. Not in this age, not in the age to come. Every conceivable authority – whether it's Caesar on his throne, or the CEO in the boardroom, or the principal spiritual forces that influence nations – all of it, under His feet.

The phrase "under His feet" – that's victory language from Psalm 110. In the ancient Near East, conquering kings would literally place their feet on the necks of defeated enemies. But notice what Jesus does with this absolute authority. He doesn't crush. He gives eternal life.

Here's something I find particularly striking: Jesus prays for this authority to be revealed. Not granted – He already has it. Revealed. Made visible. Made known. And He's praying this for His disciples, which includes you and me! He wants us to know, really know, that He has authority over everything human.

Think about what that means for a moment. That difficult person in your leadership sphere? Jesus has authority over them. That impossible situation with seemingly immovable human obstacles? Jesus has authority over it. That government official, that board member, that influencer, that critic? Under His feet. Not eventually. Now.

But – and this is crucial – we often miss how this authority operates. It's not like earthly authority that dominates and demands. When Pilate boasted about his power to crucify or release Jesus, our Lord responded, "You would have no power over me if it were not given to you from above" (John 19:11). Even Pilate's authority to crucify was under Christ's authority! Jesus submitted to the cross not from weakness but from a position of ultimate authority.

The early church grasped this in ways that changed history. When they stood before governors and emperors, they weren't standing before ultimate authority. They were standing before people under Jesus' feet. Not in an arrogant "we're better than you" way, but with the quiet confidence that comes from knowing who really holds "all authority in heaven and on earth".

I remember reading about Polycarp, that early church leader, being threatened with death if he didn't renounce Christ. His response? "Eighty-six years I have served Him, and He has done me no wrong. How can I blaspheme my King who saved me?" That's not the response of someone who thinks earthly authority is ultimate. That's someone who knows what Jesus prayed for us to know – He has authority over all people.

And here's the beautiful paradox: the more we recognise Christ's authority over all people, the more humbly we exercise our own leadership. We're not trying to establish our kingdom; we're serving under His authority. We're not building our empire; we're participating in His rule.

Every human authority you encounter today – your boss, the government, the culture-shapers, even your own leadership role – it all exists under Jesus' authority. No name, no power, is exempt from His rule. Not one.

LIVING IT OUT

Today, take a mental inventory of the human authorities that feel overwhelming in your life or leadership. Write them down if it helps. Then, deliberately place each one "under His feet" – not in contempt, but in proper perspective. That intimidating board member? Under Jesus' authority. That government regulation? Under His feet. That cultural pressure? Subject to His rule. Now approach your day differently. You're not navigating independent power structures; you're moving through a world where Jesus has authority over all people. Let this reshape how you pray, how you lead, and how you respond to human authority. You serve the One to whom all authority has been given.

PRAYER

Lord Jesus, You prayed for us to see Your authority clearly, and sometimes I'm so blinded by earthly power structures that I forget. No name is exempt from Your rule – what a magnificent truth!

Help me remember today that every human authority I encounter operates under Your supreme authority. Give me the humble confidence that comes from knowing I serve the One who has authority over all people. May this transform how I lead, how I follow, and how I navigate the complex web of human relationships and power. You are Lord of all. Amen.

TOMORROW'S PREVIEW

We weren't designed for fear – it wasn't in God's original blueprint for humanity. Tomorrow, we'll explore why every single fear we experience is actually evidence that we're living in a story that's already been rewritten by Christ's victory.

DAY 4

Foreign to Our Design

"The LORD God called to the man, 'Where are you?' He answered, 'I heard you in the garden, and I was afraid because I was naked; so I hid.'" (Genesis 3:9-10)

"For God has not given us a spirit of fear, but of power and of love and of a sound mind." (2 Timothy 1:7 NKJV)

REFLECTION

"I was afraid."

Those are the first recorded words of human fear in all of Scripture. Think about that. Adam lived in perfect paradise – naming animals, walking with God, enjoying unbroken intimacy with his Creator – and the word "afraid" never crossed his lips. Until sin entered.

Fear wasn't part of the original operating system, if you will. God didn't install it. It's a virus that came with the Fall.

DAY 4

Neuroscientists have discovered something fascinating about fear. When we experience it, our amygdala hijacks our brain in about 12 milliseconds. That's faster than our conscious thought, which takes about 25 milliseconds. We literally fear before we think. But here's the remarkable bit – they've also found that perfect love, deep trust, actually calms the amygdala. It's as if our brains still carry the memory of Eden, where perfect love meant no fear.

You know what Adam was doing when fear first gripped him? Hiding. And we've been hiding ever since, haven't we? Behind titles, behind success, behind carefully curated images, behind theological degrees, behind leadership positions. Fear drives us into sophisticated hiding places.

But consider this: every fear you've ever experienced is proof that you're living in a fallen world, not the world God designed for you. Fear of failure? Didn't exist in Eden – there was nothing to fail at when everything was "very good". Fear of rejection? Impossible when you're fully known and fully loved. Fear of death? Death wasn't even a concept until sin entered.

Here's what absolutely captivates me though: Jesus, the second Adam, lived thirty-three years as a human being and never once operated from fear. Storms? He slept through them. Crowds trying to throw Him off a cliff? He walked right through them. Crucifixion looming? He set His face like flint towards Jerusalem.

How?

Because He was living from humanity's original design, not its fallen state. He showed us what humans look like when they're not infected with fear's virus. And then – this is the spectacular bit – He went to the cross to destroy the very source of fear: sin and death.

I was reading recently about cliff divers in Acapulco. They dive from heights of up to 35 metres, but here's the crucial detail – they have to time their dive perfectly with the waves or they'll hit water that's too shallow. The difference between life and death? About 3 seconds. Yet these divers don't operate from fear. They operate from trained confidence, precise knowledge, and complete trust in their preparation.

That's rather like what Christ has done for us, isn't it? He's removed the ultimate danger – eternal death – so now we can dive into life without fear controlling us. We still need wisdom, certainly. We still need preparation, absolutely. But fear? That's not supposed to be our operating system anymore.

Paul tells Timothy that God hasn't given us a spirit of fear. The Greek word there is "deilia" – it means timidity, cowardice. It's the kind of fear that makes you shrink back from your calling. God didn't give us that spirit because He never intended us to need it. It's foreign to our original design.

Instead, He's given us power – "dunamis" – the same word used for dynamite. Love – "agape" – the same love that cast out fear in Eden. And a sound mind – "sophronismos" – self-discipline, self-control, the ability to think clearly without fear's fog.

Every time fear rises up in your leadership – fear of making the wrong decision, fear of confrontation, fear of failure, fear of not being enough – remember this: that fear is evidence that you're not home yet. It's proof that this broken world isn't your natural habitat. You were designed for Eden, destined for the New Jerusalem, where fear simply doesn't exist.

But here's the glorious truth: Christ's victory means fear's days are numbered. It's already a defeated enemy, even if it doesn't feel like it. Like those last Japanese soldiers who kept fighting World War II for decades because they didn't know it was over, fear keeps fighting even though Christ has already won the war.

LIVING IT OUT

Identify your most persistent fear in leadership right now. Name it specifically. Then ask yourself: "Would this fear have existed in Eden?" Of course not. Now ask: "Will this fear exist in the New Jerusalem?" Absolutely not. This fear is temporary, sandwiched between two fear-free realities. Today, when that fear surfaces, don't just try to be brave.

Remember that fear itself is foreign to your true design. You're not overcoming something that's supposed to be there; you're rejecting something that was never meant to exist. Practise responding from your original design – power, love, and a sound mind – rather than from fear's false narrative.

PRAYER

Father, You designed me for a world without fear, and every anxious thought reminds me that I'm not home yet. Thank You that through Christ, fear's defeat is certain, even when it feels overwhelming.

Help me to remember that fear is not my friend, not my guide, and certainly not my master; it's an invader that Christ has already conquered. Today, when fear whispers its lies, let me respond from my original design: power, love, and clarity of mind. I'm not made for fear; I'm made for fellowship with You. Amen.

TOMORROW'S PREVIEW

OBEY – four letters that might just spell out the secret to spiritual authority: Ordered, Burning, Earnest, Yearning. Tomorrow we'll unpack why obedience isn't about rules but about love set on fire.

DAY 5

O.B.E.Y

"Jesus replied, 'Anyone who loves me will obey my teaching. My Father will love them, and we will come to them and make our home with them.'" (John 14:23)

"His commands are not burdensome, for everyone born of God overcomes the world." (1 John 5:3-4)

REFLECTION

God gave me this peculiar download recently about the word OBEY. Four letters that unpacked themselves like a divine acronym: Ordered - Burning - Earnest - Yearning.

Let me explain, because this completely revolutionised how I understand obedience.

Ordered. Not ordered as in commanded, but ordered as in arranged, structured, purposeful. Like a garden rather than a wilderness. When I obey God, my life moves from chaos to cosmos – that beautiful Greek word meaning an orderly arrangement. The opposite of chaos isn't control; it's order. Divine order.

I think of an orchestra warming up – that cacophony of individual instruments doing their own thing. Then the conductor raises the baton, and suddenly there's order. Every instrument still plays its unique part, but now there's harmony, purpose, beauty. That's what obedience does. It doesn't silence our individuality; it arranges it into something magnificent.

Burning. True obedience is never cold compliance. It burns. Moses' bush burned but wasn't consumed. The disciples on the Emmaus road said, "Were not our hearts burning within us?" (Luke 24:32). There's a holy fire in genuine obedience that mechanistic rule-following never produces.

The Hebrew word for "offering" – "korban" – comes from the root meaning "to draw near". Every burnt offering in the Old Testament was about drawing near through burning. When we obey with burning hearts rather than grinding duty, we're not just following rules – we're drawing near to the consuming fire Himself.

Earnest. This isn't casual obedience, the kind where we tick boxes while our hearts are elsewhere. Earnest means sincere, intense, showing depth of feeling. The Greek word "spoudaios" carries the sense of speed, diligence, earnestness all wrapped together – like someone running towards something they desperately want, not away from something they fear.

Peter writes about "earnest prayer" and "earnest love" – the same quality belongs in our obedience. Not the earnestness of trying to earn something, but the earnestness of someone who's tasted and seen that the Lord is good and wants more.

Yearning. This surprised me most. Obedience contains yearning? Absolutely. The psalmist writes, "As the deer pants for streams of water, so my soul pants for you, my God" (Psalm 42:1). That's yearning. And genuine obedience springs from that same deep place.

You see, we've got obedience backwards. We think it's about restraining our desires, when actually it's about having our deepest desires met. Augustine said our hearts are restless until they rest in God. Obedience is how restless hearts find rest. It's yearning finding its home.

C.S. Lewis wrote something that haunts me in the best way: "It would seem that Our Lord finds our desires not too strong, but too weak. We are half-hearted creatures, fooling about with drink and sex and ambition when infinite joy is offered us." True obedience isn't about wanting less; it's about wanting more – wanting what we were actually made for.

When these four elements combine – Ordered, Burning, Earnest, Yearning – obedience transforms from burden to beauty. It's no longer about gritting our teeth and doing the right thing. It's about our whole being aligned with its Creator, burning with holy passion, earnestly pursuing, yearning for more of Him.

Think about a river flowing towards the sea. Is the river "obeying" when it follows its banks? Or is it simply being what it was created to be, flowing towards its destination with all the force of gravity and nature behind it? The banks don't restrict the river; they direct its power.

That's biblical obedience. Not restriction but direction. Not limitation but liberation. Not less life but more life – abundant life, actually.

Jesus said something remarkable: "My Father will love them, and we will come to them and make our home with them." That's the promise attached to love-driven obedience. The Trinity takes up residence. Not visits. Makes their home.

Can you imagine? Your obedience creates a dwelling place for the Divine. Not your perfection – that's impossible.

Not your performance – that's exhausting. Your ordered, burning, earnest, yearning response to Love Himself.

LIVING IT OUT

Take one area where obedience feels like mere duty right now – perhaps a leadership responsibility, a spiritual discipline, or a relational commitment. Now run it through the OBEY filter. How could you bring Order to it rather than chaos? What would it look like if your heart was Burning rather than cold? How can you approach it with Earnest intention rather than half-hearted compliance? What holy Yearning might God be awakening through this obedience? Today, transform one act of dutiful obedience into OBEY – let it be ordered, burning, earnest and yearning. Watch how this shifts not just your actions but your entire spiritual atmosphere.

PRAYER

Lord Jesus, forgive me for reducing obedience to reluctant compliance when You meant it to be a burning response to Love. Transform my duty into delight, my compliance into communion. Let my obedience be Ordered

– bringing Your cosmos to my chaos; Burning – alive with holy fire; Earnest – sincere and whole-hearted; Yearning – reaching for more of You. Make Your home in my obedience today. I don't just want to do what You say; I want to want what You want. Set my obedience ablaze. Amen.

TOMORROW'S PREVIEW

At the start of this year, God gave me one word: recalibration. Tomorrow, we'll explore how God keeps adjusting our measurements, realigning our gauges, and why spiritual recalibration might be the most important leadership skill nobody taught you.

DAY 6

Recalibration

"Do not conform to the pattern of this world, but be transformed by the renewing of your mind. Then you will be able to test and approve what God's will is – his good, pleasing and perfect will." (Romans 12:2)

"Search me, God, and know my heart; test me and know my anxious thoughts. See if there is any offensive way in me, and lead me in the way everlasting." (Psalm 139:23-24)

REFLECTION

Recalibration.

That's the word God dropped into my spirit at the beginning of this year, and it's been reverberating through everything since. Not revision. Not renewal. Recalibration.

Let me tell you why this matters so profoundly.

My friend who's a pilot explained something fascinating to me. Even the most sophisticated aircraft, with all their computerised navigation systems, drift off course. A flight from London to New York, if it never recalibrated, would end up hundreds of miles off target – possibly in the Atlantic Ocean. The instruments aren't failing or losing precision; it's the environment itself that introduces small deviations. Factors like wind, air pressure, and magnetic variation gradually push the aircraft away from its intended path.

The solution? Constant recalibration. Checking position against fixed points. Adjusting. Realigning. Not because the pilot is incompetent, but because drift is inevitable in a world of variables.

That's exactly what happens to us spiritually, especially in leadership. We don't suddenly wake up one day completely off course. We drift. Our measurements subtly shift. What felt like sacrifice last year feels like entitlement this year. What seemed like bold faith gradually becomes presumption. What started as healthy confidence slides towards pride.

The world around us is constantly recalibrating our instruments to its frequencies. Success gets redefined by metrics that have nothing to do with the Kingdom. Leadership gets measured by influence rather than servanthood. Growth means numbers rather than depth. We don't even notice it happening.

Here's what struck me about that word "recalibration" – it assumes your instruments are worth saving. You don't recalibrate something that's broken; you replace it. You recalibrate something that's valuable but needs adjustment. God wasn't telling me I was broken. He was telling me I needed realignment.

In precision engineering, recalibration happens against an absolute standard. They have these blocks of metal – gauge blocks – that are so precisely manufactured they're accurate to millionths of an inch. Everything else gets measured against these unchanging standards.

For us? Christ is our gauge block. Unchanging. Precise. Absolute. We recalibrate against His life, His words, His way.

But here's what really got me – recalibration requires humility. You have to admit your measurements might be off. You have to be willing to discover you've been using the wrong scale. Sometimes what you thought was ten units of faith turns out to be two units of faith and eight units of presumption.

I've been learning to pray David's dangerous prayer: "Search me, God." That's inviting divine recalibration. It's saying, "Check my measurements. Test my gauges. Show me where I've drifted."

And He does! Sometimes it's gentle – a Scripture that suddenly reads differently, a conversation that shifts perspective, a quiet conviction during prayer. Sometimes it's more dramatic – a failure that reveals pride, a conflict that exposes selfishness, a disappointment that uncovers misplaced trust.

Professional musicians constantly tune their instruments. Not just at the beginning of a concert, but between movements, sometimes between songs. The temperature in the concert hall, the humidity, the very act of playing – everything pulls the instrument slightly off pitch. The best musicians are the ones who never stop listening for drift, never stop adjusting.

That's what God was asking of me this year. Stay tuneable. Stay adjustable. Keep checking your pitch against the perfect frequency of heaven.

You know what's interesting? In the Old Testament, they had to recalibrate their calendar regularly because the lunar year didn't match the solar year. Without adjustment, Passover would eventually drift into autumn. So they'd add an extra month when needed. An entire month! That's major recalibration. But it kept their worship aligned with God's timing.

Some of us need that kind of major recalibration. We've been measuring ministry by worldly metrics for so long, we need to add whole new categories to our assessment. Others just need minor adjustments – a degree here, a percentage there.

The beautiful thing about spiritual recalibration? It's not about perfection; it's about position. Are you positioned to hear? Positioned to adjust? Positioned to realign? That's all He's asking.

LIVING IT OUT

Choose one area of your leadership that feels "off" lately – perhaps your motivations feel murky, your priorities feel scrambled, or your peace has evaporated. That's drift. Today, bring that specific area to God for recalibration. Ask Him three questions: "What am I measuring that You're not measuring? What am I not measuring that You are measuring? What standard am I using that isn't Yours?" Then listen. Really listen. Be prepared to discover your measurements need significant adjustment. Write down what you hear. This isn't about condemning yourself for drift; it's about gratefully accepting realignment. Everyone drifts. Leaders simply have the courage to recalibrate.

PRAYER

Master Craftsman, I've been using the world's measuring tape while claiming to build Your Kingdom. Recalibrate me. Show me where my definitions have drifted, where my standards have shifted, where my instruments need adjustment. I want to measure success by Your metrics, growth by Your standards, faithfulness by Your gauge.

Give me the humility to accept correction and the wisdom to maintain alignment. Keep me tuneable, Lord. Don't let me drift so far that I can't find my way back to true. You are my fixed point, my true north, my unchanging standard. Align me afresh today. Amen.

TOMORROW'S PREVIEW

We're terrible at remembering – our minds leak like sieves. Yet God keeps giving us ways to remember what matters most. Tomorrow, we'll discover why forgetfulness might be our biggest enemy and remembrance our greatest weapon.

DAY 7

Remember to Remember

"Only be careful, and watch yourselves closely so that you do not forget the things your eyes have seen or let them fade from your heart as long as you live." (Deuteronomy 4:9)

"Do this in remembrance of me." (Luke 22:19)

REFLECTION

I nearly forgot our wedding anniversary once!

Not deliberately, mind you. It just . . . slipped away. Like water through fingers. My wife, gracious as she is, found it more amusing than offensive, but it taught me something profound about the human condition: we're absolutely terrible at remembering what matters most.

Scientists tell us we forget 50 per cent of new information within an hour. After 24 hours? 70 per cent is gone. After a week? We're lucky to retain 10 per cent. Our minds really are like those kitchen sieves – everything important just drains through unless we actively work to retain it.

But here's what fascinates me: God knows this about us. He designed us, after all. And throughout Scripture, He's constantly building in memory aids, recurring rituals, physical reminders. He's like a loving parent who knows their child will forget their lunch money, so they stick notes everywhere.

Take the Israelites. Twelve stones from the Jordan River, piled up at Gilgal. "When your children ask you, 'What do these stones mean?' tell them . . ." (Joshua 4:6-7). God literally told them to heap up rocks because He knew they'd forget that miraculous river crossing. Without those stones, within a generation it would become myth, then legend, then nothing.

The Passover meal – every single year, the same story retold. Why? Because God knows that even the most dramatic deliverance – plagues, parted seas, pillars of fire – will fade from memory like morning mist. So He institutes an annual remembrance. Taste the bitter herbs. See the blood on the doorpost. Remember.

Those phylacteries the Orthodox Jews wear, with Scripture literally strapped to their foreheads and arms? That comes from Deuteronomy: "Tie them as symbols on your hands and bind them on your foreheads" (6:8; 11:18). God essentially said, "You're going to forget my words, so literally strap them to your body."

And then Jesus, at the last supper, knowing full well our leaky-sieve minds, doesn't give us a theology to memorise or a creed to recite. He gives us bread and wine. "Do this in remembrance of me." Every time you eat, remember. Every time you drink, remember. He hijacks our most basic, repeated human activities and transforms them into memory triggers.

Why? Because forgetting is perhaps our greatest spiritual danger.

The Israelites forgot God's miracles and made a golden calf – while Moses was still on the mountain receiving the Ten Commandments! Peter forgot Jesus' prediction and denied Him three times. The church at Ephesus forgot their first love. We forget answered prayers, forget deliverances, forget provisions, forget promises.

Some keep what I call a "remembrance journal". Not a diary, exactly. Just a record of when God showed up. That impossible situation that resolved. That provision that came from nowhere. That word that proved true. They've discovered something humbling – we can worship passionately on Sunday for what God did, and by Wednesday, we're anxious about the future as if He's never come through before.

The Hebrew word "zakar" – to remember – appears 233 times in the Old Testament. It's not passive recollection; it's active, deliberate, intentional calling to mind. It's fighting against forgetting.

You know what's remarkable? When we take communion, we're joining an unbroken chain of remembrance stretching back two thousand years. Every generation of believers, in every nation, through persecution and prosperity, has lifted bread and cup saying, "We remember." We're terrible at remembering individually, but collectively, through ritual and rhythm, we've remembered.

Modern technology was supposed to help us remember everything. We've got phones that store thousands of photos, cloud storage that never forgets, social media that shows us "memories" from years ago. Yet somehow, we're more forgetful than ever about what truly matters. We remember the trivial and forget the transcendent.

But God, in His kindness, keeps giving us remembrance opportunities. Sunday worship – weekly remembrance.

Christmas and Easter – annual remembrance. Baptisms, testimonies, celebrations – communal remembrance. He knows our minds leak, so He keeps refilling them.

That's why the Psalms constantly say "I will remember". Not "I do remember" but "I will remember" – future tense, intentional, deliberate. It's a choice, a discipline, a holy rebellion against our forgetful nature.

(These days, we plan a date night out (as a minimum) to celebrate our anniversary!)

LIVING IT OUT

Create a physical remembrance trigger today. It could be a stone on your desk from a place where God met you. A photo on your phone's lock screen of a moment when God provided. A bracelet, a bookmark, a Post-it note with a date when God showed up. Something tangible that fights against forgetting. Then, choose one story of God's faithfulness in your life and tell it to someone today. Not a sermon, just a simple "Let me tell you about a time when God . . ." Because remembering alone is good, but remembering together is powerful. We're leaky sieves individually, but together we can hold the water of remembrance.

PRAYER

Lord, I confess I'm a chronic forgetter. I forget Your faithfulness while staring at my fears. I forget Your provision while calculating my problems. I forget Your promises while dwelling on my circumstances. Thank You for knowing this about me and providing so many ways to remember.

Help me build monuments of remembrance in my life – not from pride but from gratitude. Teach me to tell the stories, keep the traditions, celebrate the moments. May my life become a collection of remembrance stones that testify: God was here. God provided. God is faithful. I will remember. Amen.

TOMORROW'S PREVIEW

Information, education, revelation – three levels of receiving truth. Tomorrow we'll discover why you can have all the information, even the education, but still miss the revelation that changes everything.

DAY 8

Information vs Revelation

"He opened their minds so they could understand the Scriptures." (Luke 24:45)

"But when he, the Spirit of truth, comes, he will guide you into all the truth." (John 16:13)

REFLECTION

Three men can look at the same ocean. The first sees water – that's information. The second understands H_2O, salinity levels, tidal patterns – that's education. The third sees the fingerprint of God, hears the echo of "Let the waters be gathered", feels the same power that parted the Red Sea – that's revelation.

All three are looking at the same ocean. But only one is truly seeing.

I've been pondering this progression lately, particularly because we live in the Information Age. Never in human history have we had access to so much data. I can pull up the original Greek text of any Bible verse in seconds. I can watch sermons from theologians across the globe. I can access centuries of commentary with a few clicks.

And yet . . . are we more spiritually mature? Are we walking in greater power? Are we seeing more transformation?

Information is facts. It's knowing that David killed Goliath. Education is understanding – the historical context, the significance of single combat in ancient warfare, the theological implications of God using the smallest to defeat the greatest. But revelation? Revelation is suddenly seeing your own Goliath through David's eyes, feeling the weight of that smooth stone in your hand, knowing in your bones that the battle is the Lord's.

The Pharisees had information. Boy, did they have information! They had memorised vast portions of Scripture. They knew every jot and tittle of the law. The Scribes had education – they could parse every word, debate every interpretation, explain every complexity. But when Revelation Himself stood before them, they missed Him entirely.

Meanwhile, fishermen with barely any formal education were receiving revelation that would transform the world.

Here's what troubles me: we've turned discipleship into information transfer. We measure spiritual growth by how much people know. We pile up Bible studies, sermons, conferences, podcasts – more information, more education. But Paul warns us that "knowledge puffs up" (1 Corinthians 8:1). It inflates without transforming.

The two on the road to Emmaus knew all the information about the Messiah. They could probably quote the prophecies. But it wasn't until Jesus "opened their minds" that revelation came. One moment they're dejected, confused disciples. The next, their hearts are burning within them. Same information, but now revelation!

Scientists have discovered something intriguing about learning. Information goes to the prefrontal cortex – our reasoning centre. Education builds neural pathways, creates connections. But transformative moments – what we might call revelation – actually involve the entire brain lighting up at once, including the emotional centres, the memory centres, even the motor cortex. It's as if our whole being suddenly knows something, not just our mind.

Peter had information about Jesus. He'd been educated by walking with Him for three years. But at Caesarea Philippi, when he declared, "You are the Christ, the Son of the living God," Jesus' response was telling: "Flesh and blood has not revealed this to you, but My Father who is in heaven" (Matthew 16:16-17 NKJV). That was revelation, and on that revelation, Jesus said He'd build His church.

Not on information. Not on education. On revelation.

The beautiful thing about revelation is that it's not earned through study or achieved through effort. It's received. It's a gift. The Holy Spirit takes what we know about God and makes us know God. There's a universe of difference between those two.

I think about Mary sitting at Jesus' feet while Martha served. Martha had the information – guests need food. She had the education – how to be a proper hostess. But Mary was receiving revelation, and Jesus said she'd chosen the better part.

We're drowning in Christian information. We're increasingly educated about spiritual things. But revelation? That requires something different. It requires stillness when we prefer productivity. It requires humility when we prefer expertise. It requires waiting when we prefer controlling.

You can inform someone in minutes. You can educate them in months or years. But revelation? That happens in moments, and it changes everything. One word from God, truly heard, truly received, carries more transformative power than a library of information.

LIVING IT OUT

Take one piece of biblical information you know well – perhaps John 3:16, the story of the Prodigal Son, or the fruit of the Spirit. You have the information. You probably have the education about it. Now, ask the Holy Spirit for revelation. Sit with it quietly. Don't study it; wait on it. Ask: "Lord, what are You wanting to reveal to me through this that I've never seen?" Don't rush. Don't force. Simply wait with expectancy. When revelation comes – and it often comes as a sudden "knowing", a fresh seeing, an unexpected connection – write it down immediately. Then watch how that revelation begins to transform not just what you know but how you live.

PRAYER

Spirit of Truth, I confess I've often settled for information about You when You're offering revelation of You. I've collected facts when You're offering encounter. I've pursued education when You're offering transformation.

DAY 8

Open my mind like You did for those disciples. Take the information I've gathered and breathe revelation into it. I don't just want to know about You; I want to know You. Not just understand Your ways but walk in them. Move me from information through education into revelation. Light up my whole being with the knowledge of You. Amen.

TOMORROW'S PREVIEW

Truth, love, and timing – the three-legged stool of godly communication. Tomorrow we'll explore why having two without the third can actually cause more damage than staying silent.

DAY 9

The Triangle of Communication

"Instead, speaking the truth in love, we will grow to become in every respect the mature body of him who is the head, that is, Christ." (Ephesians 4:15)

"To every thing there is a season, and a time to every purpose under the heaven . . . a time to keep silence, and a time to speak." (Ecclesiastes 3:1,7 KJV)

REFLECTION

Picture a three-legged stool. Remove any leg, and the whole thing collapses. That's exactly how godly communication works: Truth, Love, and Timing. All three, or it doesn't stand.

I learned this the hard way when I once told someone a hard truth – absolutely accurate, completely necessary – but I did it publicly, in front of others, at the worst possible moment. I had truth, arguably even love (I wanted them to grow), but my timing was catastrophic. The message that could have brought life brought devastation instead.

Truth without love is brutality. We've all met that person who prides themselves on "telling it like it is", leaving wounded souls in their wake. They're right, but they're not righteous. They win arguments but lose people. Like a surgeon operating without anaesthetic – technically accomplishing the task but causing unnecessary agony.

Love without truth is sentimentality. It's watching someone head towards a cliff and saying nothing because we don't want to upset them. It feels kind in the moment but it's actually cruel in the long run. Like giving sugar water to a diabetic because we want them to enjoy something sweet.

But here's the one we often miss: perfect truth spoken in perfect love but at the wrong time? That's stillborn wisdom. It dies before it can bring life.

(Here's my favourite example of great feedback!) Nathan the prophet understood this triangle perfectly when confronting David about Bathsheba. He didn't burst into the throne room the moment he heard about the sin. He waited. He prepared. He crafted a parable about sheep. When he finally spoke, he had all three: truth (David's sin), love (desire for restoration), and timing (when David's heart was ready to hear). The result? Genuine repentance and the most honest psalm ever written – Psalm 51.

Jesus was the master of this triangle. With the woman caught in adultery, notice His timing – He writes in the dirt first, creating space, letting tempers cool. Then truth: "Go and sin no more." Wrapped in love: "Neither do I condemn you" (see John 8:1-11). Perfect triangle.

But watch Him with the Pharisees. Sometimes He answers immediately with scorching truth. Sometimes He responds with a question. Sometimes He stays silent. Same truth, same love, different timing for different hearts.

Proverbs says, "A word fitly spoken is like apples of gold in pictures of silver" (Proverbs 25:11 KJV). That word "fitly" in Hebrew means "upon its wheels" – suggesting something that rolls smoothly, arrives at the right moment, perfectly timed. Not forced, not pushed, but rolling naturally into place.

I think of a midwife delivering a baby. She knows the truth – this baby needs to be born. She has love – for both mother and child. But if she forces the timing, she could cause terrible damage. Too early is dangerous. Too late is dangerous. There's a window, a season, a moment when everything aligns.

The triangle also applies to receiving communication. Sometimes we receive truth but miss the love behind it, so we feel attacked rather than cared for. Sometimes we feel the love but resist the truth, so we stay comfortable but unchanged. And sometimes the timing is premature – we're not ready to hear what we desperately need to hear.

Farmers understand this instinctively. You can have the best seed (truth) and the richest soil (love), but if you plant in the wrong season (timing), you get nothing. The seed isn't wrong. The soil isn't wrong. The timing is everything.

In our instant-communication age, we've largely lost the timing leg of this stool. We tweet our truths immediately. We text our feelings instantly. We respond in the heat of the moment. We've confused immediacy with importance, speed with significance.

But Kingdom communication follows heaven's calendar, not earth's clock. There's a time to speak immediately – when someone's about to step into traffic. There's a time to wait years - like God did with Abraham before giving him Isaac.

How do we know the timing? That's where the Holy Spirit comes in. He's called the Spirit of Truth – He knows what needs to be said. He's poured out God's love in our hearts – He knows how it needs to be said. And He exists outside of time while operating within it – He knows when it needs to be said.

LIVING IT OUT

Think of a conversation you need to have – perhaps a difficult truth that needs speaking, or an encouragement that needs sharing. Now, honestly evaluate your triangle. Do you have the facts straight (truth)? Is your heart genuinely seeking their good, not your vindication (love)? Have you prayed about the timing – not just "should I?" but "when?" If any leg is wobbly, wait. Strengthen what's weak. If you're unsure about timing, here's a practical test: are you pushing this conversation or is God opening a door for it? Today, practise the discipline of complete communication – ensuring all three legs are strong before you speak. Remember: partial obedience in communication (two legs instead of three) is still disobedience.

PRAYER

Lord Jesus, You perfectly embodied the triangle of communication – always true, always loving, always perfectly timed. I confess I often speak with only one or two legs of this stool. Sometimes I'm truthful but loveless. Sometimes I'm loving but not truthful. Often, I completely ignore Your timing. Teach me to wait when I want to rush, to speak when I want to hide, to love when I want to be right. Give me Your heart for truth, Your motivation of love, and Your sensitivity to timing. May my words be like apples of gold in pictures of silver – beautiful, valuable, and perfectly placed.

TOMORROW'S PREVIEW

Your body either responds to medicine or reacts to it – and there's a world of difference between the two. Tomorrow we'll discover why the same is true spiritually, and why knowing the difference might save your ministry.

D A Y 10

Respond, Don't React

"Everyone should be quick to listen, slow to speak and slow to become angry." (James 1:19)

"A gentle answer turns away wrath, but a harsh word stirs up anger." (Proverbs 15:1)

REFLECTION

My doctor friend explained something that completely shifted how I think about spiritual health. When you take medicine, your body does one of two things: it responds or it reacts. They sound similar, but they're opposites.

A response means the medicine is doing what it's supposed to do – healing, restoring, bringing balance. A reaction? That's your body rejecting it, fighting it, treating it as a threat. Hives, swelling, anaphylaxis – that's not healing, that's war.

The same medicine. Two completely different outcomes. One brings life; the other could bring death.

This is exactly what happens with truth in our spiritual lives. The same word from God, the same correction, the same opportunity – one person responds, another reacts. And the difference determines whether we grow, or blow up!

Think about King Saul and King David. Both were confronted by prophets about their sin. Saul reacted – he made excuses, shifted blame, eventually tried to kill the messenger. David responded – "I have sinned against the Lord." Same medicine of correction, opposite outcomes. One lost the kingdom; one became a man after God's own heart.

Reactions are immediate, instinctive, defensive. They come from our amygdala – that ancient part of our brain that's all about survival. Fight or flight. No thought, just explosion or escape. When someone gives us feedback and we immediately start defending ourselves before they've even finished speaking? That's reaction.

Responses are considered, processed, chosen. They engage our prefrontal cortex – the part capable of wisdom, reflection, seeing bigger pictures. There's a pause, however brief, between stimulus and action. Viktor Frankl called this pause "the last of human freedoms" – the ability to choose our response regardless of circumstances.

Jesus never reacted. Not once. Think about that. Accused falsely? He responded with silence or truth, never reaction. Struck on the face? He responded with dignity, not retaliation. Peter cutting off the ear of the high priest's servant? Jesus responded with healing, not escalation.

Even on the cross – the ultimate provocation – "Father, forgive them" is a response, not a reaction. It required engaging His will, His love, His divine nature. A reaction would have been calling down twelve legions of angels.

In medicine, allergic reactions often get worse with repeated exposure. First time might be mild itching. Second time, hives. Third time, throat closes. The body becomes increasingly sensitised, increasingly reactive.

Same with spiritual reactions. The first time someone challenges our leadership, we might just be mildly defensive. But if we keep reacting instead of responding, we become increasingly allergic to correction. Eventually, we can't receive even gentle feedback without explosive reaction.

I've noticed something fascinating in the Gospels. The disciples often reacted – "Call down fire from heaven!" "Send the crowds away!" "Forbid them!" But three years with Jesus slowly transformed their reactions into responses. By Acts, these same hot-headed men are responding to persecution with joy, to threats with prayer, to problems with wisdom.

What changed? The Holy Spirit. He's called the Comforter, the Counsellor – literally, the One who comes alongside. He creates that pause between stimulus and action. He gives us time to choose response over reaction.

Here's the diagnostic test: reactions leave you feeling justified but isolated. You won the argument but lost the relationship. You proved your point but poisoned the well. Responses leave you feeling peaceful, even if the situation isn't resolved. You maintained integrity even if you didn't maintain control.

In leadership, this might be the most critical skill. Every day brings provocations – criticism, disappointment, betrayal, failure. If we react to all of it, we'll spend our ministry in defensive mode, allergic to the very feedback that could refine us.

But if we learn to respond? That criticism becomes data for growth. That disappointment becomes opportunity for faith. That betrayal becomes occasion for forgiveness. Same medicine, but now it's healing instead of harming.

The apostle Paul gives us the prescription: "Be slow to speak, slow to anger." That slowness isn't weakness; it's the pause that transforms reaction into response. It's the deep breath that engages wisdom instead of wounding.

LIVING IT OUT

Today, you'll face at least one situation that tempts reaction – an annoying email, a cutting comment, an unfair situation. When it comes, practise the holy pause. Before you speak, before you type, before you act, take one deep breath and ask: "Is this a reaction or a response?" If it's a reaction (defensive, immediate, emotionally-driven), stop. Wait. Pray. Transform it into a response. It might help to write out your reaction privately first – get it out of your system – then craft your actual response. Notice how different they are. That gap between reaction and response? That's where spiritual maturity lives. Today, choose to respond to at least one situation where you'd normally react.

PRAYER

Lord Jesus, You showed us what perfect response looks like – never reactive, always redemptive. I confess I'm often allergic to the very medicine You're using to heal me. I react to correction, to criticism, to challenges. Teach me the holy pause. When everything in me wants to react, give me the grace to respond. Let Your Spirit create that space between stimulus and action where wisdom can flourish. Transform my spiritual allergies into spiritual health. May I become someone who responds with grace rather than reacts with grievance. Amen.

TOMORROW'S PREVIEW

Are you being careful or full of care? They sound the same but lead to completely different destinations – one to anxious self-protection, the other to thoughtful stewardship. Tomorrow we'll untangle these twins and discover which one you're actually living.

DAY 11

Careful or Full of Care

"Do not be anxious about anything, but in every situation, by prayer and petition, with thanksgiving, present your requests to God." (Philippians 4:6)

"Cast all your anxiety on him because he cares for you." (1 Peter 5:7)

REFLECTION

The English language plays tricks on us sometimes. "Careful" – we use it as a compliment. "She's so careful with the details." But break it down: care-full. Full of care. Stuffed with anxiety. Brimming with worry.

Is that really what we want to be?

I've been wrestling with this distinction because I've noticed something in my own leadership. When I think I'm being "careful" – prudent, wise, thorough – I'm often actually being "full of care" – anxious, controlling, fearful. They masquerade as the same thing, but they flow from completely different springs.

Being careful, in its truest sense, means being thoughtful, attentive, diligent. It's Joseph storing grain for seven years because God revealed a coming famine. That's wisdom in action. But being full of care? That's Joseph lying awake every night for seven years, anxiously checking the grain stores, worried the dream was wrong, stressed about a thousand what-ifs.

One is stewardship; the other is anxiety wearing a responsible costume.

Jesus addressed this directly with Martha. She was careful – preparing, serving, managing all the details. But Jesus said she was "worried and upset about many things" (Luke 10:41). She wasn't just being diligent; she was full of care. Mary, sitting at Jesus' feet, might have looked careless to Martha, but she was actually practising true carefulness – attending to what mattered most without anxiety.

The Greek word for anxiety – "merimnao" – literally means to be divided, to be pulled apart. When we're full of care, our minds fracture into a thousand pieces, each one worrying about a different outcome. We're not integrated; we're disintegrated.

True carefulness, biblical thoughtfulness, keeps us whole. We plan like it depends on us and trust like it depends on God. We're diligent without being anxious, thorough without being threatened.

In John 10 Jesus teaches us about the difference between a shepherd and a hired hand. Both might watch the sheep carefully. But the shepherd watches from love and responsibility – thoughtful, attentive, present. The hired hand watches from fear – what if I lose one? What if the owner gets angry? What if something goes wrong? Same external behaviour, completely different internal reality.

Parents know this distinction instinctively. There's a difference between watching your child play with appropriate attentiveness and hovering with anxiety. One enables growth; the other stifles it. One communicates love; the other communicates lack of trust – in the child, in God, in life itself.

Paul tells us to "be anxious for nothing". That's not carelessness – immediately after, he talks about thinking on things that are true, noble, right, pure. That requires care! But it's care without the fullness, attention without the anxiety, thoughtfulness without the threat.

The distinction becomes crystal clear in how we handle responsibility. When I'm being truly careful (thoughtful), I prepare well, execute faithfully, then rest in the results. When I'm full of care (anxious), I over-prepare, second-guess every decision, and lie awake regardless of the outcome.

Here's what I've discovered: being full of care is actually prideful. It assumes the universe rests on my shoulders. It believes my worry somehow contributes to the outcome. It trusts my anxiety more than God's sovereignty.

True carefulness is humble. It acknowledges my responsibility while recognising God's ultimate control. It does what's mine to do, then releases what's His to handle.

The Sabbath principle teaches this perfectly. Work six days – be careful, thoughtful, diligent. Then rest. If you can't rest, you're not being careful; you're full of care. You're not trusting your thoughtful work; you're trusting your anxious energy.

Watch how Jesus lived. He was incredibly careful – choosing disciples thoughtfully, teaching with precision, timing His revelations perfectly. But He was never full of care. He slept in storms. He withdrew to pray when crowds pressed. He faced the cross with resolution, not anxiety.

Peter instructs us to cast our anxiety on God because He cares for us. Beautiful wordplay there – we give Him our care-fullness, and He gives us His care. We trade our fractured worry for His integrated love.

LIVING IT OUT

Examine your calendar for next week. Where are you being careful (thoughtfully planning, wisely preparing) and where are you being full of care (anxiously over-controlling, fearfully micro-managing)? Choose one area where anxiety has dressed itself up as responsibility. Now practise true carefulness: prepare what you can, plan what you should, then deliberately release the outcome to God. Write down exactly what you're responsible for and what God is responsible for. Do yours. Leave His. Tonight before bed, if you find yourself full of care about tomorrow, remind yourself: "I've been careful (thoughtful). I refuse to be full of care (anxious). I cast this care on the One who cares for me."

PRAYER

Caring Father, I confess I've confused being full of care with being faithful. I've worn anxiety like a badge of responsibility. I've trusted my worry more than Your sovereignty. Teach me the difference between thoughtful stewardship and anxious control. Help me be careful without being care-full, diligent without being divided, responsible without being wrecked with worry. You care for me perfectly – let me rest in that care instead of carrying cares You never asked me to bear. Show me how to work like everything depends on me, then sleep like everything depends on You. Because it does. Amen.

TOMORROW'S PREVIEW

Have you ever noticed the arrow hidden in the FedEx logo? Once you see it, you can't unsee it. Tomorrow we'll discover what that arrow teaches us about spiritual perception and why some people see Kingdom realities that others completely miss.

DAY 12

The Hidden Arrow

"The disciples came to him and asked, 'Why do you speak to the people in parables?' He replied, 'Because the knowledge of the secrets of the kingdom of heaven has been given to you, but not to them.'" (Matthew 13:10-11)

"Open my eyes that I may see wonderful things in your law." (Psalm 119:18)

REFLECTION

Right there, between the E and the x in FedEx, lives a perfect white arrow pointing forward. Been there since 1994. Millions see that logo every day on trucks, packages, planes. Most never notice the arrow.

But once you see it? You can't unsee it. Every FedEx truck becomes a rolling revelation. That arrow was always there, hiding in plain sight, waiting to be discovered.

The designer, Lindon Leader, spent months crafting it. He said he wanted to communicate forward movement, speed, precision. But he hid it. Not buried it – hid it. There's a difference. Buried things are meant to stay hidden. Hidden things are meant to be found.

This is exactly how the Kingdom of God operates.

Jesus said He spoke in parables so that "seeing they do not see" (Matthew 13:13). That used to trouble me. Why would Jesus hide truth? But He wasn't hiding it from seekers; He was hiding it from casual observers. The treasure was there for anyone willing to look beyond the surface.

The religious leaders of Jesus' day saw His miracles, heard His teaching, witnessed His life. They saw the letters, so to speak, but missed the arrow. Meanwhile, tax collectors and fishermen were seeing Kingdom realities everywhere – in mustard seeds, in pearls, in wedding feasts.

What made the difference? The position of their hearts determined the perception of their eyes.

I've discovered this principle operates constantly in Scripture. The star over Bethlehem was visible to countless astronomers. Only the Magi saw it as divine GPS. Five thousand ate the multiplied loaves. Only the disciples saw the sign pointing to the Bread of Life.

There's always more than meets the eye – if we have eyes to see.

Corporate culture experts say the FedEx arrow works because of "negative space" – the space between things that creates something new. That's profound. Sometimes what's not there reveals more than what is. The gaps tell the story.

Consider the genealogy of Jesus in Matthew. Most people see a boring list of names. But look at the gaps, the negative space. Four women mentioned – all with scandalous stories. Tamar, Rahab, Ruth, Bathsheba. The arrow pointing forward says: God uses broken people, outsiders, the unexpected. It was always there, waiting to be seen.

Or take the four hundred years of silence between Malachi and Matthew. We call them the "silent years". But were they? Or was God writing an arrow in the negative space, building anticipation, creating hunger, so that when John the Baptist cried "Prepare the way!" people were ready?

Elisha's servant saw an army surrounding them and panicked. Elisha saw the invisible army of God filling the mountains. Same landscape, different perception. Elisha prayed, "Open his eyes, LORD" (2 Kings 6:17) and suddenly the servant saw the arrows that were always there – flaming chariots, heavenly warriors, divine protection.

That prayer – "Open his eyes" – it wasn't about giving the servant new information. It was about giving him new perception. The heavenly army didn't suddenly appear; it was suddenly seen.

This is why some people can sit through powerful worship and remain unmoved while others are undone. Why one person reads Scripture and sees rules while another sees relationship. Why one leader sees problems while another sees possibilities. They're looking at the same thing, but only one sees the arrow.

The Emmaus road disciples walked with Jesus for miles without recognising Him. Their eyes were "kept from recognising him" (Luke 24:16) – not blindfolded, just unable to perceive. Then, in the breaking of bread, "their eyes were opened" (v. 31). The arrow appeared. Same Jesus, new perception.

Modern brain science tells us we literally see what we expect to see. Our brains filter out millions of bits of information, only processing what we deem relevant. Change what you're looking for, and you'll change what you see.

Paul prays for the Ephesians to have "the eyes of your heart enlightened" (Ephesians 1:18). Not informed – enlightened. Not educated – illuminated. He's praying for them to see the arrows that are already there: the hope of His calling, the riches of His inheritance, the incomparable greatness of His power.

LIVING IT OUT

Choose something familiar today – your workplace, your church, a relationship, even a problem you're facing. Now look for the arrow. What's God doing in the negative space? What's He revealing between the obvious? Ask Him specifically: "Lord, what have I been looking at but not seeing? What arrow have You hidden in plain sight?" Then pay attention. Look for patterns you've missed, provisions you've overlooked, purposes hiding in problems. When you find your arrow (and you will, if you look), share it with someone. Help them see what you've discovered. Remember: the arrow in FedEx was designed to be found. So are God's Kingdom realities in your everyday life.

PRAYER

Lord, I've been looking at my life like most people look at the FedEx logo – seeing the obvious, missing the miraculous. Open my eyes to see the arrows You've hidden in plain sight. Give me perception, not just information. Help me see what You're doing in the negative spaces, in the gaps, in the silence.

I want to see Your Kingdom breaking through in places I've overlooked. Transform me from a casual observer to a treasure hunter, always looking for the more You've embedded in the mundane. Show me the arrows, Lord. Once I see them, I'll never unsee them. Amen.

TOMORROW'S PREVIEW

Athletes know the secret: without challenge, there's no change. Tomorrow we'll discover why your greatest ministry breakthrough might be hiding inside your biggest current challenge – if you're willing to embrace the resistance.

DAY 13

No challenge, No Chance

"Consider it pure joy, my brothers and sisters, whenever you face trials of many kinds, because you know that the testing of your faith produces perseverance." (James 1:2-3)

"No discipline seems pleasant at the time, but painful. Later on, however, it produces a harvest of righteousness and peace for those who have been trained by it." (Hebrews 12:11)

REFLECTION

Any serious athlete will tell you about progressive overload. If you bench press 50 kilograms every day for a year, you'll maintain your strength but never increase it. The muscles adapt, settle, stop growing. Want to get stronger? Add weight. Create challenge. Force adaptation.

The muscle fibres actually tear under the strain – microscopic damage that sounds terrible but is actually the whole point. During recovery, they rebuild stronger than before. No challenge, no tears. No tears, no growth. No growth, no change.

God runs our spiritual development on exactly the same principle.

When the Israelites left Egypt, God could have taken them straight to the Promised Land – about an eleven-day journey. Instead? Forty years of wilderness. Why? "Remember how the LORD your God led you all the way in the wilderness these forty years, to humble and test you in order to know what was in your heart" (Deuteronomy 8:2).

Testing. Challenge. Resistance. Not as punishment but as training.

Professional marathon runners train at high altitudes where oxygen is scarce. Their bodies adapt by producing more red blood cells. When they return to sea level, they have a massive advantage – their bodies are overbuilt for the conditions. The challenge at altitude creates capacity for the race.

Jacob wrestled with God all night and walked away limping. That limp wasn't a failure; it was a trophy. He was renamed Israel – "he who struggles with God". His descendants would carry that name forever. The challenge didn't diminish him; it defined him.

DAY 13

We tend to pray for ease when God is providing exactly what we need – resistance training for the soul.

Paul begged God three times to remove his thorn in the flesh. God's response? "My grace is sufficient for you, for my power is made perfect in weakness" (2 Corinthians 12:9). The challenge Paul wanted removed was the very thing producing spiritual strength he couldn't get any other way.

Sports scientists have discovered that muscles grow during rest, not during exercise. The workout creates the stimulus, but growth happens in recovery. Same principle spiritually – God brings challenge, then gives grace for recovery, and in that cycle, we grow.

But here's what we miss: not all challenge brings change. Destructive challenge breaks down without building up. It's the difference between training and injury, between pruning and hacking.

A good trainer pushes you just beyond comfort but not into damage. They know when to add weight and when to reduce it. They understand periodisation – cycles of stress and recovery. God is the perfect trainer. Every challenge He allows is measured, purposeful, designed for growth not destruction.

DAY 13

The three Hebrew boys in the furnace – the challenge was extreme, but notice: they walked around in the fire. They weren't consumed, weren't even singed. The only things that burned were their bonds. The challenge freed them rather than destroyed them!

Modern neuroscience shows our brains operate the same way as muscles – they need challenge to grow. Neuroplasticity, they call it. Learn a new language, tackle complex problems, break routine patterns – the brain literally rewires itself, creates new pathways, becomes more capable. Comfort leads to cognitive decline. Challenge creates cognitive enhancement.

Why do we think spiritual growth would be different?

Timothy was young, naturally timid. Paul didn't coddle him. He challenged him: "Fan into flame the gift of God . . . For the Spirit God gave us does not make us timid" (2 Timothy 1:6-7). Paul knew Timothy needed challenge to catalyse change.

Even Jesus "learned obedience from what he suffered" (Hebrews 5:8). Perfect God in human flesh still grew through challenge. The wilderness temptation, Gethsemane, the cross – each challenge produced something necessary for His mission.

Here's the diagnostic question: when did you last do something that required faith? Not preference, not comfort, but actual faith? If you can accomplish everything in your current capacity, you're not growing. You're maintaining.

Comfort zones aren't comfortable – they're stagnant. They feel safe but they're actually dangerous, like still water that becomes a breeding ground for disease. Running water stays fresh precisely because it keeps moving, keeps encountering resistance, keeps being challenged by rocks and rapids.

LIVING IT OUT

Identify the challenge you're currently resisting or resenting. Maybe it's a difficult person, an impossible deadline, a resource limitation, a leadership struggle. Now reframe it: this isn't an obstacle to your ministry; it's equipment for your development.

What capacity is this challenge trying to build? What spiritual muscle is under load? Today, instead of praying for the challenge to be removed, pray for the strength to be increased. Ask God: "What are You developing in me through this resistance?" Then lean into it like an athlete embraces the burn. Document what you're learning – maybe keep a "challenge journal" where you track the correlation between resistance faced and capacity gained. Remember: the very challenge you're avoiding might be the equipment for the breakthrough you're seeking.

PRAYER

Divine Trainer, forgive me for constantly seeking comfort when You're offering transformation. I've been praying for lighter weights when You're trying to build greater strength.

Help me embrace challenge as gift, resistance as resource, testing as training. Show me the difference between destructive difficulty and constructive challenge. Give me the courage to stay under the load long enough for change to happen. When everything in me wants to quit, remind me that muscles grow in the burn, faith grows in the fire, and leaders grow in the challenge. Thank You for loving me too much to leave me comfortable. Amen.

TOMORROW'S PREVIEW

A fat chance and a slim chance mean exactly the same thing – how's that for confusing?! Tomorrow we'll explore

DAY 13

how God uses completely opposite circumstances to teach us identical lessons, and why that should revolutionise how we interpret our experiences.

DAY 14

Fat Chance, Slim Chance

"I know what it is to be in need, and I know what it is to have plenty. I have learned the secret of being content in any and every situation, whether well fed or hungry, whether living in plenty or in want." (Philippians 4:12)

"To the weak I became weak, to win the weak. I have become all things to all people so that by all possible means I might save some." (1 Corinthians 9:22)

REFLECTION

The English language is wonderfully mad sometimes. A fat chance and a slim chance mean exactly the same thing – virtually no chance at all! Overlook and oversee should be similar, but they're opposites. You fill in a form by filling it out.

But these linguistic quirks reveal something profound about how God teaches us.

DAY 14

Joseph learned about God's sovereignty through slavery and through ruling. Opposite circumstances, identical lesson. The pit taught him what the palace reinforced – God is in control. Prison and power were different classrooms for the same curriculum.

Consider Paul's education in contentment. "I have learned the secret," he says. What secret? That completely opposite conditions can produce identical spiritual formation. Plenty and want, full and hungry, abundance and need – all teaching the same lesson: Christ is sufficient.

We think God uses consistent circumstances to teach consistent truths. But He's far more creative than that.

Elijah encountered God in the dramatic – fire from heaven, ravens bringing bread, raising the dead. Then at Mount Horeb, in the gentle whisper. Opposite experiences, same God. The God of the spectacular and the God of the subtle. Both revealing His nature, just through contrasting means.

Peter learned about faith by walking on water (supernatural success) and by sinking in it (natural failure). Both experiences taught him the same thing – keep your eyes on Jesus. The triumph and the terror were teaching identical truths.

This explains why two Christians can have completely opposite experiences and both grow closer to God. One gets healed; another stays sick. One receives miraculous provision; another learns through lack. One has their prayer answered yes; another answered no. Fat chance, slim chance – same spiritual development.

Job's friends couldn't grasp this. They believed prosperity meant God's favour and suffering meant God's judgment. Simple equation, logical correlation. But Job's story shattered that formula. His suffering and his eventual restoration taught the same lesson – God is sovereign, God is good, God is worthy of worship regardless.

The Beatitudes mess with our categories completely. Blessed are the poor and blessed are those who hunger for righteousness. Blessed are the mourners and blessed are the peacemakers. Jesus is saying opposite conditions can produce identical blessedness.

We see this in church history. The church exploded during persecution under Rome. The church also exploded during the peace of Constantine. Opposite circumstances, same Kingdom advancement. God used both the catacombs and the cathedrals.

DAY 14

Modern missionaries report the same phenomenon. In some places, miraculous signs and wonders open hearts. In others, quiet acts of service over decades. Some fields see harvest through confrontation with darkness; others through patient dialogue. Fat chance, slim chance – gospel advances.

The danger is when we absolutise our own experience. "God always provides at the last minute!" says someone who's experienced that. But their neighbour experienced God's provision through careful planning and savings. Both provisions, different methods. "God speaks to me through dreams!" Wonderful. He speaks to another through Scripture study. Both hearing, different frequencies.

David wrote psalms in caves running from Saul and in palaces ruling Israel. The cave psalms and the palace psalms both worship the same God. His circumstances changed dramatically; his revelation of God only deepened.

This is liberating, actually. It means there's no circumstance outside God's curriculum. Promotion or demotion – both can teach humility. Marriage or singleness – both can teach devotion. Success or failure – both can teach dependence.

The Pharisees couldn't understand how tax collectors and religious leaders could both need salvation. They saw opposite people, not identical need. Jesus saw through the opposite exteriors to the identical interior – all needing grace.

Watch how Jesus trained the disciples. Sometimes He explained everything clearly. Sometimes He left them completely confused. Sometimes He included them in miracles. Sometimes He did miracles without them. Opposite methods, identical goal – making them fishers of men.

The key is asking the right question. Not "Why this circumstance?" but "What's the lesson?" Not "Why opposite to others?" but "What's the identical truth God is teaching?"

LIVING IT OUT

Think of someone whose life circumstances are opposite to yours right now – they're in abundance while you struggle, or they're facing hardship while you prosper. Now identify one spiritual lesson God is teaching both of you through your opposite situations. Perhaps it's trust, or gratitude, or dependence, or courage.

Reach out to that person today and share this insight: "I think God is teaching us the same thing through opposite circumstances." Compare notes on how God uses fat chances and slim chances to accomplish identical spiritual formation

This conversation will revolutionise how both of you interpret your experiences. Stop comparing circumstances; start comparing lessons.

PRAYER

Creative God, You're not limited by circumstances – You use all things, even opposites, to accomplish Your purposes. Forgive me for envying others' situations or despising my own, not realising You're teaching the same truths through different means.

Help me see past the fat or slim of my chances to the identical lessons You're teaching. Whether in plenty or want, success or failure, clarity or confusion, may I learn what You're teaching.

Thank You that no circumstance is wasted, no situation is outside Your curriculum. You're the God of the mountains and valleys, teaching the same truths from different elevations. Open my eyes to the lesson, not just the circumstance. Amen.

TOMORROW'S PREVIEW

Wine connoisseurs speak of "terroir" – how soil, climate, and history create unique flavour. Tomorrow we'll discover how God uses the terroir of your life, including the difficult soil, to produce something that could come from nowhere else.

DAY 15

Your Terroir

"But we have this treasure in jars of clay to show that this all-surpassing power is from God and not from us." (2 Corinthians 4:7)

"I am the vine; you are the branches. If you remain in me and I in you, you will bear much fruit." (John 15:5)

REFLECTION

French winemakers have a word that's almost sacred to them: terroir. It's untranslatable, really. It means the complete natural environment in which a wine is produced – the soil, the climate, the slope of the hill, the surrounding plants, even the particular yeasts floating in the air. Everything that makes that specific vineyard unique.

Here's what captivates me: you can take the exact same grape variety, plant it in two different regions, follow identical winemaking processes, and produce completely different wines. Why? Terroir. The soil speaks through the grape.

Volcanic soil from Mount Etna produces wines with a distinctive minerality. Limestone from Chablis creates that famous flinty taste. The slate soils of Spain's Priorat region give their wines a particular character. The grape is the same; the terroir makes it unique.

But it goes deeper than chemistry. Great terroir often comes from difficult soil. The best wines don't come from rich, fertile ground where vines grow easily. They come from poor soil where vines must struggle, sending roots down 30, 40, sometimes 60 feet searching for water and nutrients.

That struggle, that stress, concentrates the flavours. Easy soil makes bland wine.

You are God's terroir.

Your particular combination of experiences, struggles, victories, failures, personality, gifts, wounds, and healing creates a unique expression of God's grace that could come from nowhere else. Your testimony has a flavour that mine doesn't. My expression of Christ has notes that yours lacks. That's not inadequacy; that's terroir.

Paul understood this. "We have this treasure in jars of clay." The treasure is the same – the gospel of Christ. But the clay vessels are different. And somehow, mysteriously, the particular composition of your clay affects how the treasure is displayed.

Consider Moses – Egyptian palace education, forty years in wilderness, speech impediment, reluctant leader. That specific terroir produced a unique expression of God's deliverance. Could God have used someone else? Of course. But the Exodus has Moses' fingerprints all over it. His particular soil affected the flavour of freedom.

Peter – impulsive fisherman, denier turned apostle, passionate and flawed. His terroir produced letters full of hope through suffering, written by someone who knew both failure and restoration intimately. You can taste his story in his words.

Paul – Pharisee, persecutor, Roman citizen, scholar. That complex terroir created someone who could argue in synagogues, quote Greek poets, claim Roman rights, and plant churches across cultures. His soil spoke through his ministry.

Here's what wine teaches us: you can't fake terroir. Wine experts can taste whether a wine truly comes from where it claims. There's an authenticity that can't be manufactured.

Same with spiritual influence. People can taste whether your ministry comes from real soil or artificial flavouring.

Your hardest ground might be producing your best fruit. That difficult childhood, that professional failure, that health crisis, that broken relationship – that's not contaminated soil to be hidden. That's terroir to be transformed.

The limestone of your disappointments creates a particular kind of wisdom. The volcanic ash of your explosive failures produces a distinctive grace. The slate of your hard experiences gives your compassion a quality others recognise but can't replicate.

Winemakers have learned something profound: they can't change their terroir, so they learn to express it. They don't try to make their volcanic soil taste like limestone. They discover what their particular terroir can uniquely produce and lean into it.

Some Christians spend their entire lives trying to have someone else's testimony, someone else's gifts, someone else's expression of faith. But God isn't interested in clones. He's the master vintner who planted you in your specific soil for a reason.

Your depression gives your joy a depth that easy happiness never could. Your doubt gives your faith a tested quality that untested belief lacks. Your weakness gives your strength a flavour that self-sufficiency never achieves.

Even the history of your soil matters. In wine, they talk about "old vines" – some over a hundred years old. These vines produce less fruit, but what they produce has incredible concentration and complexity. They carry the memory of decades in their fruit.

Your history – generational blessings and curses, family patterns broken and continued, cultural heritage embraced and transcended – it's all terroir. It all speaks through your fruit.

LIVING IT OUT

Today, stop apologising for your terroir and start appreciating it. Make a list of five difficult "soils" in your life – hard experiences, challenging backgrounds, persistent struggles. Next to each, write what unique flavour this has added to your faith. What can you offer because of (not despite) this difficult ground? How has this terroir made your expression of God's grace unique? Then identify one person who needs exactly what your particular terroir has produced. Share your story with them – not the sanitised version, but the real soil, the actual struggle, the authentic flavour. They don't need generic encouragement; they need the specific vintage only your terroir can produce.

PRAYER

Master Winemaker, thank You for planting me in my particular soil – even the rocky, difficult, painful parts. I've spent too much time wishing for different terroir instead of recognising what You're producing through mine. Help me see that my struggles aren't contamination but concentration, my history isn't handicap but unique flavour. Show me how to express, not hide, the terroir You've given me. May my life produce a vintage of grace that could come from nowhere else, telling a story that only my soil can tell. You are the vine, I am the branch, and my particular soil is speaking through the fruit. Let it speak of Your redemption. Amen.

TOMORROW'S PREVIEW

"If you can be offended, you will be offended!" Tomorrow we'll explore why offence is not just possible but inevitable, and how to develop spiritual immunity to this universal leadership poison.

DAY 16

If You Can Be Offended

"Great peace have those who love your law, and nothing can make them stumble." (Psalm 119:165)

"A brother wronged is more unyielding than a fortified city; disputes are like the barred gates of a citadel." (Proverbs 18:19)

REFLECTION

"If you can be offended, you will be offended!"

When I first heard that years ago, I thought the speaker was being cynical. Now I recognise it as one of the most practical prophetic warnings I've ever received. It's not pessimism; it's spiritual physics. Like saying, "If you can get wet, and you stand in the rain long enough, you will get wet."

Here's the mathematics of it: in leadership, you'll make thousands of decisions. You'll have hundreds of interactions. You'll communicate countless times. Even if you get it right 99 per cent of the time, that 1 per cent will offend someone.

And that's assuming you get it right 99 per cent of the time, which, let's be honest, none of us do!

Add to that equation: people will misunderstand your motives, mishear your words, misinterpret your actions. They'll project their pain onto your decisions. They'll filter your leadership through their wounds. If you can be offended, the opportunities are literally endless.

Jesus warned us about this. He called offence "skandalon" – it's where we get our word scandal. But the original Greek meant the trigger of a trap, the stick that springs the snare. Offence is the enemy's trap, and the bait is always our pride.

Think about it – what actually gets offended in us? Not our spirit, which is secure in Christ. Not our new nature, which is hidden with God. It's always our ego, our reputation, our sense of fairness, our need to be understood, appreciated, validated. The flesh is infinitely offendable because the flesh is infinitely insecure.

Jesus modelled perfect unoffendability. Accused of being demon-possessed? He kept teaching. Religious leaders plotting His death? He kept healing. His own hometown rejected Him? He simply moved on to the next town. Judas betraying Him with a kiss? "Friend, do what you came to do" (Matthew 26:50 ESV).

How? He had nothing to protect. His identity was secure in the Father. His reputation was the Father's business. His vindication would come from above, not around.

John the Baptist could have been offended when Jesus' ministry overshadowed his. His disciples were: "Rabbi, everyone is going to him!" But John understood: "He must increase, but I must decrease" (John 3:30 NKJV). When you're already decreasing by choice, you can't be offended by being decreased.

Here's what I've observed: offence is cumulative. Rarely does someone leave a church or quit a position over one big offence. It's usually dozens of small offences, carefully collected, meticulously catalogued, regularly reviewed. Like a collector of grievances, building their case for eventual departure.

Proverbs says a brother offended is harder to win than a fortified city. Have you ever tried to reconcile with someone who's been collecting offences? Every attempt at resolution is met with another stored grievance. The walls get higher, the gates more barred. They've become imprisoned in their own fortress of offence.

But here's the strangest part: we often treasure our offences. We polish them like trophies. We share them like credentials. "Let me tell you what they did to me . . ." becomes our testimony. We've confused being wounded with being wronged, being hurt with being heroic.

The early church father John Chrysostom said something profound: "It is not he who reviles or strikes you who injures you, but your opinion of these things as being injurious. When anyone provokes you, know that it is your own opinion that provokes you."

That's hard to swallow, isn't it? But it's true. The offence doesn't happen in their action; it happens in our reaction. They pull the trigger, but we choose whether to let the trap spring.

Love keeps no record of wrongs, Paul says. That's not just nice poetry; it's practical immunity. If you're not keeping score, you can't be offended by the score. If you're not collecting debts, you can't be bitter about unpaid bills.

I've watched too many leaders shipwreck on the reef of offence. They had the calling, the gifting, the anointing – but they could be offended. And eventually, inevitably, they were. The trap sprang. The ministry ended. Not because of sin or failure or lack of vision, but because of offence.

Here's the diagnostic test: what would it take to offend you? Not being appreciated? Being misunderstood? Overlooked for promotion? Criticised unfairly? Your ideas rejected? Your sacrifice unnoticed? Whatever your answer, that's your vulnerability. That's where the trap is set.

LIVING IT OUT

Today, conduct an offence audit. What offences are you currently carrying? Not the big dramatic ones – the small, persistent irritations. Who hasn't appreciated you properly? Who misunderstood your intentions? Who overlooked your contribution? Write them down. All of them. Then do something radical: forgive each one, specifically, by name.

Not because they deserve it, but because you deserve freedom. Those offences you're carrying? They're not badges of honour; they're chains of bondage.

Then go further: identify your "offence triggers" – what consistently offends you? That's where you need to pre-decide your response. When (not if) it happens again, you'll be ready to let it go rather than let it grow.

PRAYER

Unoffendable Saviour, You showed us it's possible to live above offence, to walk through this world without collecting wounds. I confess I'm infinitely offendable because I'm still protecting my ego, my reputation, my rights.

Free me from the need to be understood, appreciated, validated by people. Secure my identity so firmly in You that offence finds no foothold. When the trigger is pulled, help me refuse to let the trap spring. Show me that offence is always a choice, and give me the grace to choose freedom instead. May I become so dead to self that there's nothing left to offend. Amen.

TOMORROW'S PREVIEW

The early church was accused of turning the world upside down. When's the last time anyone accused you of that? Tomorrow we'll rediscover what world-overturning faith actually looks like and why we've settled for so much less.

DAY 17

Upside Down

"These men who have turned the world upside down have come here also." (Acts 17:6 ESV)

"And they overcame him by the blood of the Lamb and by the word of their testimony, and they did not love their lives to the death." (Revelation 12:11 NKJV)

REFLECTION

"These men who have turned the world upside down!"

That wasn't a compliment. That was an accusation, shouted by angry civic leaders in Thessalonica. Paul and Silas had been in town for maybe three weeks. Three weeks! And the city authorities were already panicking about a complete social upheaval.

When did we stop being dangerous to the status quo?!

Seriously, when was the last time anyone accused the church of turning anything upside down? We've become so respectable, so predictable, so . . . safe. We fit neatly into society's expectations. We threaten no systems, challenge no powers, disturb no peace. We've traded our revolutionary birthright for a bowl of cultural acceptance.

The early church didn't have buildings, budgets, or political influence. They had no social media strategy, no marketing department, no celebrity endorsements. What they had was the explosive power of transformed lives and the audacious claim that Jesus, not Caesar, was Lord.

That was enough to terrify empires.

Think about the sheer audacity of it. Twelve working-class men from a backwater province of Rome, following a crucified carpenter, claiming He'd risen from the dead and was now running the universe. Within three centuries, they'd conquered the empire that crucified Him. Not with swords but with love. Not with politics but with sacrifice.

They turned economics upside down – sharing everything, eliminating poverty among themselves. They turned social structures upside down – slaves and masters eating together, Jews and Gentiles worshipping together, women prophesying alongside men. They turned religion upside down – no temple needed, no priestly class required, direct access to God for everyone.

No wonder the authorities were terrified.

But here's what strikes me: they weren't trying to be revolutionary. They were just being obedient. They weren't strategising disruption; they were simply living out the Kingdom. The world-upending was a by-product of the life-living.

When we really follow Jesus – not culturally, not nominally, but actually follow Him – we can't help but turn things upside down. Or rather, right-side up. Because what the world calls normal, heaven calls broken. What culture calls success, Kingdom calls failure. What society calls wisdom, God calls foolishness.

The Roman Empire had a saying: "Caesar is Lord." It was their pledge of allegiance, their national motto. Christians had a different saying: "Jesus is Lord." Those three words were treason. They undermined the entire power structure of the known world. And Christians said them anyway, even when it meant lions and crosses and flames.

Today we've made Christianity so compatible with culture that nobody feels threatened. We've taught a Jesus who improves your life but doesn't overturn it. We've preached a gospel that makes you nice but not new. We've built churches that make good citizens but not dangerous disciples.

When Paul preached in Ephesus, the silversmiths rioted because conversions were destroying the idol business. When did ministry last threaten someone's profit margin? When early Christians entered a city, fortune-tellers went bankrupt, brothels lost customers, and gladiatorial games lost spectators. When we enter a city, property values might go up slightly.

The accusation was specifically that they "turned the world upside down". The Greek word is "anastatoo" – to upset, to unsettle, to make tumultuous. It's the same root as "anastasis" – resurrection. There's a linguistic link between resurrection and revolution. What raises the dead disturbs the living.

Modern historians estimate the entire Christian population at the end of the first century was maybe 25,000 people. Some would say that's a decent-sized church today. Yet those 25,000 had the Roman Empire strategising about how to stop them. We have millions of Christians, and the world barely notices except when we're fighting among ourselves.

What happened? We stopped believing the Kingdom was real. We started treating it as metaphor instead of reality. We made peace with systems Jesus came to overthrow. We sought influence in the very power structures the cross exposed as bankrupt.

The early church prayed for boldness, not safety. They rejoiced in persecution, not comfort. They measured success by transformation, not attendance. They changed cities, not just individuals.

Peter and John, arrested for healing a lame man, were commanded to stop speaking about Jesus. Their response? "We cannot help speaking about what we have seen and heard" (Acts 4:20). That's world-turning faith – when you literally cannot help but overflow with Kingdom reality.

LIVING IT OUT

Here's your challenge: identify one system, practice, or assumption in your sphere that's considered normal but contradicts the Kingdom. Maybe it's how success is measured at work. Maybe it's how value is assigned in relationships. Maybe it's how power operates in your community. Now, this week, deliberately live according to Kingdom economics instead of worldly wisdom in that area. Serve where others dominate. Give where others take. Include where others exclude. Love where others hate.

Don't announce it, don't trumpet it, just do it. Live so counter-culturally that people have to ask why. When they do, tell them about your upside-down King. Watch how even one person living Kingdom reality begins to destabilise status quo assumptions.

PRAYER

Revolutionary King, forgive us for domesticating Your dangerous gospel. We've made You safe when You came to make all things new. We've settled for personal improvement when You offered cosmic revolution. Resurrect in us the world-turning faith of the early church.

Make us dangerous to every system that opposes Your Kingdom. Give us the holy audacity to live as if Your Kingdom is real, because it is. May our lives be so transformed that our cities are disrupted.

May we be accused once again of turning the world upside down. Or rather, right-side up. Your Kingdom come, Your will be done, on earth as it is in heaven. Even if it costs us everything. Amen.

TOMORROW'S PREVIEW

Your mess becomes your message, your test becomes your testimony – but only if you come through them correctly. Tomorrow we'll discover how God transforms your worst chapters into your greatest authority to speak hope to others.

DAY 18

Mess to Message, Test to Testimony

"Praise be to the God and Father of our Lord Jesus Christ, the Father of compassion and the God of all comfort, who comforts us in all our troubles, so that we can comfort those in any trouble with the comfort we ourselves receive from God." (2 Corinthians 1:3-4)

"And they overcame him by the blood of the Lamb and by the word of their testimony." (Revelation 12:11 NKJV)

REFLECTION

Your mess is your message in disguise. Your test is your testimony waiting to be born.

But here's the crucial bit – it's not automatic. How you come through determines what you have to say on the other side.

A leader I know watched two people go through nearly identical divorces. One emerged bitter, cynical, closed. Their message became: "Never trust again." The other emerged broken but beautified, wounded but wise. Their message: "God restores what seems irreparable." Same mess, completely different message. The difference? How they came through.

Joseph could have emerged from thirteen years of slavery and prison with a message of vengeance. "Look what my brothers did to me! Look how I survived despite them!" Instead, he emerged with: "You intended to harm me, but God intended it for good" (Genesis 50:20). His test became a testimony of sovereignty, not survival.

The determining factor isn't the severity of the mess or the difficulty of the test. It's whether you let God into it while you're in it.

Some people go through trials and simply endure. They white-knuckle their way through, teeth gritted, heart closed, just trying to survive. They come out with war stories but no wisdom, experiences but no revelation. They can tell you what happened, but they can't tell you what it means.

Others go through the same trials and engage. They wrestle with God like Jacob. They ask the hard questions. They let their hearts break. They choose to believe when belief seems insane. They come out limping but blessed, scarred but radiant. They have authority to speak because they paid the price to learn.

Paul's thorn in the flesh could have produced a message of disappointment: "God doesn't always heal." Instead, it produced: "His grace is sufficient, His power is perfected in weakness." The difference? Paul pressed into the mystery instead of becoming disabled by it.

Here's what I've noticed: your greatest ministry will likely flow from your deepest pain – but only if you let God redeem it while you're in it. The alcoholic who finds freedom becomes the addiction counsellor. The abandoned child who finds belonging becomes the foster parent. The business failure who finds purpose becomes the life coach. But only if they came through correctly.

Coming through correctly doesn't mean perfectly. Peter denied Jesus three times – that's about as imperfect as it gets. But he let that failure break him, reshape him, recommission him. His mess of denial became a message of restoration. His test of loyalty became a testimony of grace.

The woman at the well had a mess – five husbands and living with a sixth man. But one encounter with Jesus transformed that mess into a message. She became the first evangelist to the Samaritans: "Come, see a man who told me everything I've ever done" (John 4:29). Her shame became her platform.

But watch this – she didn't hide her mess. She led with it. "He told me everything I've ever done." Your mess doesn't disqualify you from ministry; it qualifies you for a specific ministry – to those in the same mess.

The problem is we often want to hurry past our mess to get to our message. We want to skip the test and jump to the testimony. But the authority in your testimony is directly proportional to the authenticity of your test. People don't need to hear from someone who's never struggled; they need to hear from someone who struggled and found God faithful.

Moses spent forty years in the wilderness before he could lead others through it. His message of deliverance required his mess of murder and exile. His testimony of God's power required his test of inadequacy and reluctance.

Here's what determines whether your mess becomes your message: do you blame or bless? Do you become bitter or better? Do you close your heart or crack it open wider? Do you curse the darkness or light a candle? Do you shake your fist at God or fall on your face before Him?

The Prodigal Son's mess was spectacular – demanded his inheritance, squandered it on wild living, ended up eating pig food. But he "came to himself" and came home. His mess became a message about the Father's heart. But his brother, who never made a mess, had no message – just resentment.

Sometimes those without a dramatic mess resent those who have one, not realising that the mess often produces the message that changes lives. Your perfect record might actually be limiting your impact.

LIVING IT OUT

Identify your current mess or your recent test – the thing you wish wasn't part of your story. Now ask yourself honestly: how am I coming through? Am I simply enduring or am I engaging? Am I becoming bitter or better? Am I closing off or opening up? Today, make a conscious decision to invite God into the middle of your mess. Ask Him: "What's the message You're forming? What's the testimony You're building?" Then take one practical step towards coming through correctly. Maybe it's choosing forgiveness over resentment. Maybe it's choosing vulnerability over self-protection. Maybe it's choosing to share your incomplete story with someone who needs hope. Remember: your mess is someone else's miracle waiting to happen, but only if you come through it with God.

PRAYER

Redeeming God, You waste nothing – not even my messes and failures. Thank You that my worst chapters can become my greatest credentials for ministry. Help me come through correctly – not perfectly, but faithfully. When I want to hide my mess, give me courage to let You transform it into a message. When I want to skip the test, help me endure it knowing it's producing testimony. Show me that my deepest pain can become my greatest platform if I'll let You into it. May my scars become someone else's roadmap to healing. Transform my mess into a message of Your mercy. Amen.

TOMORROW'S PREVIEW

I have a button that's lost its middle cross – completely useless now. Tomorrow we'll explore what happens when we lose the cross at the centre of anything, and why that broken button might be the most important reminder in my drawer.

DAY 19

The Useless Button

"For I resolved to know nothing while I was with you except Jesus Christ and him crucified." (1 Corinthians 2:2)

"But far be it from me to boast except in the cross of our Lord Jesus Christ, by which the world has been crucified to me, and I to the world." (Galatians 6:14 ESV)

REFLECTION

I keep a broken button in my desk drawer. Four holes, no centre. The little cross-shaped piece that held the thread snapped off years ago – probably from too much strain, too much pulling in different directions. Without that centre cross, the button is completely useless. Can't attach it to anything. Can't make it functional. It's just a circular piece of plastic with nowhere to anchor.

I can't throw it away though. It preaches to me.

Everything loses its purpose when the cross disappears from the centre. Everything.

A church without the cross at its centre becomes a social club with hymns. Lovely people, meaningful friendships, shared values – but no power to transform. I've visited churches with magnificent buildings, talented musicians, eloquent preachers, efficient programmes. But somewhere along the way, the cross shifted from centre to periphery. They still had all the holes for threading ministry through, but nothing to anchor it to.

Marriage without the cross at the centre becomes a negotiation between two selfish people. You can have attraction, compatibility, shared goals, even genuine affection. But when the cross isn't the anchor point, every thread of connection eventually snaps under pressure. Two people demanding their rights instead of laying them down. Two people keeping score instead of keeping covenant.

Leadership without the cross at the centre becomes manipulation with good intentions. You might have vision, strategy, communication skills, emotional intelligence. All the holes are there for threading influence through. But without the cross – that radical model of power through sacrifice, greatness through service, life through death – leadership devolves into empire-building, even in ministry.

DAY 19

The Corinthian church had everything – spiritual gifts, knowledge, resources. Paul said they lacked no spiritual gift. But they'd lost the cross from the centre. So Paul had to remind them: "I resolved to know nothing while I was with you except Jesus Christ and him crucified." Not Jesus Christ and Him resurrected only. Not Jesus Christ and Him reigning only. Jesus Christ and Him crucified. The cross has to stay central.

Even our theology can lose its centre cross. We can have systematic precision, hermeneutical sophistication, doctrinal purity – all the holes for threading truth through. But if the cross isn't the interpretive centre, we end up with religion that binds rather than frees, academics that impress rather than transform, orthodoxy that's right but not righteous.

Personal disciplines without the cross at centre become self-improvement projects. Prayer becomes wish-list presentation. Bible study becomes information accumulation. Fasting becomes willpower demonstration. Giving becomes tax strategy. All good things, but without the cross at centre, they can't hold the weight of transformation.

The cross is scandalous precisely because it insists on being central. It won't settle for being one philosophy among many, one path among options, one truth among truths. The cross demands to be the centre that holds everything else together, or it becomes nothing at all.

Paul said something extraordinary: "Far be it from me to boast except in the cross." Not in his revelations, his church plants, his sufferings for the gospel. The cross. Because he understood that everything else derived its meaning from that centre point.

When the cross is central, success gets redefined – it looks like a grain of wheat falling into ground and dying. When the cross is central, power gets redefined – it's perfected in weakness. When the cross is central, wisdom gets redefined – it's foolishness to the perishing but power to those being saved.

Modern Christianity keeps trying to make the faith attractive by moving the cross to the edges. Make it about prosperity, happiness, self-fulfilment, social justice, political power – anything but that bloody, scandalous cross. We'll keep it as decoration, as jewellery, as architectural element. But as centre? That's embarrassing. Primitive. Off-putting.

But here's what that broken button reminds me: you can have all the right elements, all the proper holes, all the correct positioning, but without the cross at centre, nothing holds. The threads of life, ministry, relationship, purpose –

they need that scandalous cross-shaped anchor point, or they eventually snap under pressure.

The reformation cry was "sola crux" – the cross alone. Not the cross plus. Not the cross among. The cross alone. As centre. As anchor. As the gravitational force that holds everything else in orbit.

LIVING IT OUT

Examine the major areas of your life today – your ministry, your relationships, your ambitions, your daily practices. Where has the cross shifted from centre to periphery? Where are you trying to hold things together with human effort because you've lost the divine anchor?

Choose one area where the cross has been displaced. Today, deliberately re-centre it. How? By applying the cross-principle: dying to self, serving rather than being served, sacrificing rather than demanding.

If it's your marriage, ask: "How would this look if the cross was at centre?" If it's your leadership, ask: "What would change if cruciform love was my anchor?" Don't just think about it – take one concrete action that puts the cross back at centre. Die to something. Sacrifice something. Serve someone. Let the cross be functional, not just theological.

PRAYER

Crucified Saviour, forgive me for trying to build life, ministry, and relationships with the cross as decoration rather than foundation. I confess I've wanted Christianity without the scandal, transformation without the dying, resurrection without crucifixion.

Like that useless button, I've lost my centre and wondered why nothing holds together. Put the cross back at the centre of everything – my thoughts, my choices, my relationships, my ministry. May I boast in nothing except Your cross. May it be my anchor, my centre, my gravitational force. Without it, I'm just a useless button. With it, everything holds. Keep me centred on the cross. Amen.

TOMORROW'S PREVIEW

Old vines make the best wine – any vintner will tell you that. Tomorrow we'll discover why spiritual generations are meant to get better, not bitter, and how the aged roots of faith should be producing increasingly excellent fruit.

Better With Age

"They will still bear fruit in old age, they will stay fresh and green, proclaiming, 'The LORD is upright; he is my Rock, and there is no wickedness in him.'" (Psalm 92:14-15)

"Therefore we do not lose heart. Though outwardly we are wasting away, yet inwardly we are being renewed day by day." (2 Corinthians 4:16 NIV)

REFLECTION

Any vintner worth their salt will tell you: old vines make the best wine.

Not good wine. The best wine. Vines that are 50, 80, sometimes over 100 years old produce grapes with complexity, depth, and concentration that young vines simply cannot match. The French have a term for it: "vieilles vignes" – old vines. It's a mark of distinction, a promise of excellence.

Here's why: as vines age, their roots drive deeper – sometimes 30 feet down or more. They tap into water tables and mineral deposits young vines can't reach. Their yield decreases (an old vine might produce 40 per cent less fruit than a young one), but what they lose in quantity, they gain exponentially in quality. Every grape carries decades of accumulated wisdom from the soil.

So why do we assume spiritual generations should deteriorate rather than improve?

Why do we expect each generation to be less faithful, less committed, less powerful than the one before? Why do churches talk about "the good old days" as if decline is inevitable? Why do we accept spiritual entropy as normal?

The vine tells a different story. Each year, the root system expands. Each season adds rings of experience. Each harvest builds on the previous one. The vine that survives drought, disease, frost, and time doesn't just endure – it excels. Its fruit becomes more precious with each passing year.

Abraham's faith was remarkable. But Isaac inherited that faith and added to it. Jacob wrestled with God and prevailed. Joseph administered prophetic dreams and saved nations. Each generation was meant to build on the previous one's foundation, not start from scratch.

Elijah did mighty miracles. But Elisha asked for a double portion and received it. He literally performed twice as many recorded miracles as his mentor. That's the pattern – not decline but increase, not dilution but concentration.

But something shifted. We started expecting less instead of more. We began accepting that revival belongs to history, that miracles were for apostolic times, that each generation would naturally drift further from the source. We institutionalised decline.

A master winemaker from Spain once told me something profound: "The vine remembers everything. Every storm, every drought, every perfect season – it's all recorded in the wood, expressed in the fruit." The vine doesn't just age; it accumulates. It compounds. It concentrates.

What if spiritual generations are meant to work the same way? What if we're supposed to inherit not just the faith of our fathers but their breakthroughs, their revelations, their authority? What if we're meant to stand on their shoulders, not start at their beginning?

The problem is we keep cutting ourselves off from our roots. Every generation wants to reinvent rather than inherit.

We'd rather plant new vines than tend old ones. We value innovation over cultivation, fresh over aged, trendy over tested.

Young vines are vigorous. They grow fast, produce quickly, look impressive. But their fruit lacks depth. It's one-dimensional. Pleasant but not profound. It takes decades for a vine to develop the kind of character that produces truly exceptional wine.

I think about the saints who've gone before – their prayers are still rising like incense before the throne. Their faith is still speaking though they're dead. Their roots are still drawing from deep wells. We're not meant to replace them but to build on them, to inherit their depth while adding our own rings of growth.

The early church understood this. They didn't just learn about Abraham's faith; they claimed it as their inheritance. They didn't just admire Moses; they exceeded him. They didn't just remember the prophets; they fulfilled their words. Each generation was meant to produce better wine, not weaker vintage.

Why better? Because they had more to draw from. More testimonies, more revelation, more accumulated wisdom in the spiritual soil. The cloud of witnesses isn't just watching; they're part of our root system.

Here's what troubles me: we've reversed the pattern. We expect youth to carry the revival while age maintains the institution. But in the vineyard, young vines need protection, support, careful tending. Old vines? They weather anything and produce liquid gold.

The Scripture promises we'll still bear fruit in old age, stay fresh and green. Not just maintain. Not just survive. Bear fruit. Stay fresh. That's the opposite of spiritual decline – that's spiritual appreciation, like wine improving with age.

LIVING IT OUT

Today, identify one spiritual inheritance you've received but haven't valued – perhaps a prayer warrior grandmother, a faithful pastor from your youth, a spiritual tradition you've abandoned as "old-fashioned". Connect with that root system. If they're still alive, call them and ask for their deepest spiritual wisdom. If they've died, read their words, pray their prayers, learn their stories.

Then add your own ring of growth. Take their best and go further. Don't just honour their ceiling; use it as your floor. Ask God: "What did they start that I'm meant to complete? What did they plant that I'm meant to harvest?"

Remember: you're not meant to produce new wine instead of theirs but better wine because of theirs. Let your generation's vintage show the accumulated wisdom of all who came before.

PRAYER

Ancient of Days, You designed faith to improve with age, not deteriorate. Forgive us for accepting decline as normal when You intended increase. Thank You for the deep roots of faith we've inherited – the saints, martyrs, reformers, revivalists who've enriched our spiritual soil.

Help us value aged vines over young shoots, depth over speed, quality over quantity. May our generation produce the best vintage yet, not because we're better but because we're building on better.

Let us bear fruit in old age that makes young vines jealous. Show us that spiritual generations, like wine, are meant to get better with time. We want to produce a vintage worthy of the roots we've inherited. Amen.

DAY 20

TOMORROW'S PREVIEW

Trees have no pump pushing water up from the ground – they survive by releasing moisture through their leaves, creating suction that draws more in. Tomorrow, in our final devotion, we'll discover the profound secret of spiritual survival: how giving away what we have creates the very vacuum that draws in more.

DAY 21

Trees Don't Have Pumps

"Give, and it will be given to you. A good measure, pressed down, shaken together and running over, will be poured into your lap." (Luke 6:38)

"Whoever refreshes others will be refreshed." (Proverbs 11:25)

REFLECTION

There's no pump in the ground pushing water up into trees.

Think about that for a moment. A giant sequoia, 300-feet tall, needs to move hundreds of gallons of water every day from roots to crown – against gravity, with no mechanical pump. How?

Transpiration. It's breathtakingly simple and profoundly mysterious. Water evaporates from the leaves, creating negative pressure – a vacuum that pulls more water up from the roots. The tree survives by giving away what it has. The very act of release creates the suction for supply.

A single mature oak tree can transpire 40,000 gallons of water per year. That's water it pulls up and releases, pulls up and releases, in an endless cycle of receiving and giving. Stop the giving, and you stop the receiving. Close the stomata (the tiny pores in leaves), and the tree dies, not from lack of water in the ground but from inability to create the draw.

This is the Kingdom economy hidden in creation.

We think we need more coming in before we can give more away. The tree knows better. It gives away to create the very vacuum that draws more in. The release IS the mechanism for the receipt.

Scientists call it the cohesion-tension theory. Water molecules stick together (cohesion) and when pulled from above (tension from evaporation), the entire column of water moves up through the tree's vessels. But it only works if the tree keeps releasing at the top. The moment it stops giving away moisture, the whole system fails.

Jesus knew this. "Give, and it will be given to you." Not "Receive, and then you'll have something to give." The giving comes first. The giving creates the capacity for receiving.

DAY 21

I've watched churches and ministries hoard resources, waiting for "enough" before they start giving generously. They wither. Meanwhile, others give beyond reason, release beyond logic, and somehow they never run dry. They've discovered tree physics – giving creates the draw.

The Dead Sea is dead precisely because it only receives. All that Jordan River water flows in but nothing flows out. Result? The saltiest, most lifeless body of water on earth. Meanwhile, the Sea of Galilee receives the same water but gives it away, and it teems with life.

Trees don't just transpire water; they release oxygen. A mature tree produces enough oxygen for two people per year. But here's the marvel – they don't need that oxygen. They release it as waste. Their waste becomes our breath. Their giving away of what they don't need becomes essential for what we desperately need.

What if our spiritual "waste" – the overflow of worship, the excess of joy, the abundance of peace – is actually someone else's lifeline? What if what we release without thinking twice about becomes critical for someone's survival?

The tree can't see where the water comes from or where the moisture goes. It just maintains the flow. Roots in the soil, leaves to the sky, constantly cycling resources it never actually possesses, only channels.

Paul understood this: "We are hard pressed on every side, but not crushed . . . struck down, but not destroyed" (2 Corinthians 4:8-9). How? He kept transpiring hope. The pressure actually increased the flow. The harder the circumstances pressed, the more grace moved through him.

Here's what staggers me: the Amazon rainforest creates its own weather. The trees release so much moisture that they generate clouds, which produce rain, which feeds the trees. Their giving creates their receiving in a massive, self-sustaining cycle. They don't wait for rain; they make rain.

What if churches operated like rainforests? Releasing so much blessing that we create atmospheric change? Not waiting for revival but generating it through radical release?

A botanist once told me that in drought, trees with the deepest roots become conduits for trees with shallow roots. Through fungal networks, they share water and nutrients. The strong transpire for the weak. Those with deep access create draw for those without.

That's meant to be us. Our deep roots in God should create draw for others. Our transpiration of grace should water those around us who can't yet reach the deep wells.

But maybe we've become spiritual misers, carefully measuring our output, calculating our giving, protecting our resources. We've forgotten that the tree that stops transpiring is already dying, even if it looks green for a season.

The principle is universal: closed hands can't receive. Full lungs can't inhale. Clenched hearts can't love. The release creates the capacity for the receipt.

LIVING IT OUT

Today, identify what you've been holding that needs releasing. Perhaps it's forgiveness you've withheld, resources you've hoarded, gifts you've hidden, love you've rationed. Now deliberately release it. Give it away. Not cautiously but generously, like a tree transpiring thousands of gallons it will never get back.

Don't wait to feel full before you give – give to create the draw for fullness. Start a transpiration journal: document what you release each day and watch for the corresponding draw of fresh supply.

Practise Kingdom physics: the more you release at the top, the more gets drawn from the Deep. Today, be a tree that creates its own weather system through radical release.

PRAYER

Source of All Life, You designed creation to teach us Your ways – trees preaching about the power of release, showing us that giving creates receiving. Forgive me for trying to preserve what You meant to flow through me. I've been a Dead Sea when You called me to be a flowing river. Teach me to transpire grace like trees transpire moisture – naturally, constantly, generously.

Let my roots go deep enough to draw from Your infinite supply, and let my leaves release freely enough to create continuous flow. May my giving create atmospheric change around me. Show me that survival isn't about holding on but letting go. Make me a tree that refreshes others by the very act of breathing. Amen.

Journey's End, Journey's Beginning

Twenty-one days. Twenty-one glimpses of Kingdom reality hidden in plain sight.

We've walked through gardens and vineyards, observed trees and stars, wrestled with fear and faith, discovered that broken buttons preach and FedEx logos hide gospel truth. We've learned that God uses opposite circumstances for identical lessons, that old vines make the best wine, and that trees survive by giving away what they have.

But here's what I hope has shifted: your eyes.

Not just what you know but how you see. Because once you start seeing Kingdom reality breaking through everywhere – in morning light and evening meals, in corporate logos and kitchen sieves, in gravity-defying trees and gravity-defining suns – you can't unsee it. The ordinary becomes extraordinary. The mundane becomes miraculous. Everything preaches.

This isn't the end of your devotional journey; it's the beginning of a new way of perceiving. God is always speaking, always revealing, always inviting us deeper. The question isn't whether He's showing up but whether we're showing up with eyes to see, ears to hear, hearts to receive.

So go. Walk through your world differently. See the arrows in the logos, the sermons in the trees, the Kingdom in the ordinary. And remember – you're not just observing these truths; you're becoming them. A tree that transpires grace. A vine producing increasingly excellent fruit. A leader who turns worlds upside down by living right-side up.

The journey continues. The revelation never stops. Keep your eyes open.

The Kingdom of God is at hand – and it's everywhere.

740a4a27-1caf-4bfb-945b-c6b5333859b0R01